CW00545741

# A STUDY OF
# BRECONSHIRE PLACE-NAMES

# A study of
# BRECONSHIRE PLACE-NAMES

*Richard Morgan*
*R.F. Peter Powell*

© *Text: Morgan/Powell*

*Copyright © by Gwasg Carreg Gwalch 1999*
*All rights reserved. No part of this publication*
*may be reproduced or transmitted, in any form*
*or by any means, without permission.*

*ISBN: 0-86381-567-7*

*Cover design: Smala, Caernarfon*

*Cover map: Morden's Map of South Wales 1695*
*relating to Brycheiniog/Brecknock*

*First published in 1999 by*
*Gwasg Carreg Gwalch, 12 Iard yr Orsaf, Llanrwst, Wales LL26 0EH*
*☎ 01492 642031   🖷 01492 641502*
*✆ books@carreg-gwalch.co.uk   Internet: www.carreg-gwalch.co.uk*

# Acknowledgements

This book is the product of a co-operative venture of the authors but we place on record our indebtedness to Tomos Roberts, Archivist of the University of Wales, Bangor, Emeritus Professor Gwynedd O. Pierce and Dr. Hywel Wyn Owen, Reader at the University of Wales, Bangor, for their assistance in the interpretation of some of the more difficult place-names. Their contributions to the study of the place-names of Wales are known to and appreciated by many. We have also benefited considerably from the work of Stephen J. Williams and the late B.G. Charles, Bedwyr Lewis Jones, Melville Richards and Ifor Williams, and indeed many others: historians, language scholars and editors – too numerous to name – who have contributed to the study of our history and languages in Wales; from their publications we have been able to extract many of our references to past spellings and use these on which to rest many of our arguments. Any errors and omissions are, of course, our own.

# Contents

# Introduction

## The Welsh Language in Breconshire

Until recently the history of the Welsh language in Wales had received little attention from scholars and it is difficult to avoid the conclusion that part of the reason for this – particularly in regard to the early history of Welsh – was the absence of a reliable and comprehensive study of Welsh place-names. Since *A Study of Radnorshire Place-Names* (Gwasg Carreg Gwalch 1998) appeared the position in regard to place-names has begun to change, thanks to the work of Hywel Wyn Owen and the late Melville Richards[1]; the study of the history of the Welsh language too is now changing: two volumes of essays under the editorship of Geraint Jenkins have recently appeared.[2] The evidence in regard to the history of the Welsh and English languages is not plentiful and is often unreliable and anecdotal, especially for the period before 1536, which re-emphasises the importance of place-name study in Wales. As far as the Welsh and English languages are concerned, I have already made some introductory remarks on the subject in the Radnorshire volume, and I shall not repeat what is said there: many of the sources cited there are also relevant to the history of Welsh and English in Breconshire. There are, however, some important differences between the history of the languages in these counties.

The history of the languages of Breconshire before the late Middle Ages is especially difficult to write since there is so little reliable evidence. In contrast to Radnorshire there are no mentions of any English settlements in Breconshire in

---

[1]   Hywel Wyn Owen, *A Pocket Guide to the Place-names of Wales* (Cardiff 1998); Melville Richards, *Enwau Tir a Gwlad*, ed. Bedwyr Lewis Jones (Caernarfon 1998)

[2]   *The Welsh Language before the Industrial Revolution (A Social History of the Welsh Language)*, ed. Geraint H. Jenkins (Cardiff 1997), and *Language and Community in the Nineteenth Century*, ed. Geraint H. Jenkins (Cardiff 1998).

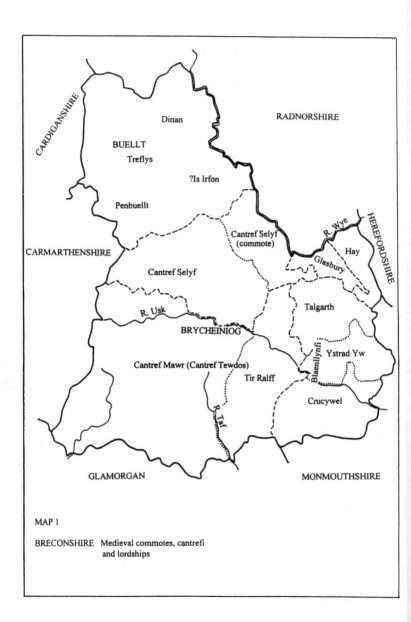

MAP 1

BRECONSHIRE  Medieval commotes, cantrefi
and lordships

8

Domesday Book 1086, though Buellt (v. Builth below) is mentioned. English may have been spoken at Glasbury – first recorded as *Clastbyrig* 1056 – and perhaps Pipton which is recorded first in the late 12thC but there are few other reliable traces in place-names. English almost certainly made its first significant impression on Breconshire in the 12thC following the conquest of Brycheiniog by Bernard de Neufmarché about 1091-93.[3] Many of the followers and military supporters of Bernard must have spoken French but their language has left no obvious trace in Breconshire's place-names except perhaps in place-names such as Trebois (Boiston).

The appearance of Anglo-Norman castles and their attendant boroughs was the main instrument in promoting English in Wales. In many boroughs the burgesses were exclusively or almost exclusively English or Anglo-French, judging by their names, especially before the mid 14thC. This seems to have been the case in Breconshire, certainly at Hay and Brecon, though the evidence is very patchy. At Brecon, for example, we know the names of a few of the early burgesses although the first substantial list does not occur until 1411 when English was in retreat: from a total of 86 burgesses only 6 were thought to bear 'unmistakeably Welsh names'.[4] The evidence of place-names is a little more revealing: we have Slwch (*Sloughe* 1566, *the Slough* 1790), almost certainly a medieval name, and the names of Brecon streets such as Ship (probably from 'Sheep') Street, Mouse Street, Free Street and Watton, though all but the last have Welsh names also, viz. Heol y Defaid, Heol y Llygoden and Heol Rhydd; note also Michael Street with its Welsh name Lôn y Popty. There are a number of field-names recorded in medieval sources such as *Keylokesmede, Annesmede, Eytlond* and *Halowmede* 1453-4[5] which again indicate English-

---

[3]  For the history of the period, v. William Rees, 'The Mediæval Lordship of Brecon', *Transactions of the Society of Cymmrodorion* 1915-16, pp. 168-175.

[4]  R.R. Davies, 'Brecon' in *Boroughs of Medieval Wales*, ed. R.A. Griffiths (Cardiff 1978), p.67.

[5]  GRO D/D CL man/box 3; v. also R.R. Davies, 'Brecon', p.56.

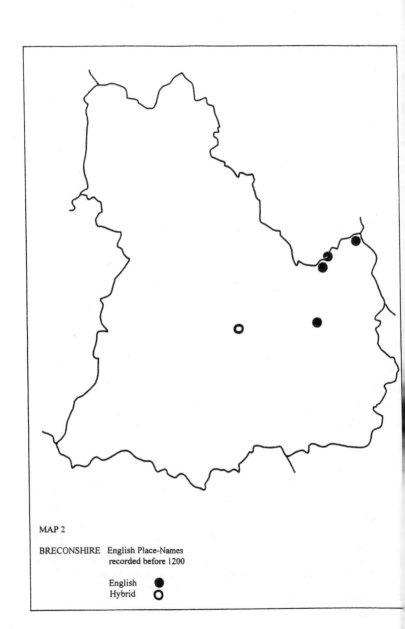

MAP 2

BRECONSHIRE   English Place-Names
recorded before 1200

English   ●
Hybrid   ○

speaking inhabitants of Brecon.

At Hay the English element in the population seems to have been more resistant to the expansion of Welsh-speaking. A survey of the lordship of Hay 1340[6] reveals that of 25 recorded burgesses not one bore a clear example of a Welsh personal-name. Place-names in the surrounding Englishry – the area subject to English law and custom – recorded in the survey include *Thomaschurche* (now Llanthomas) and a tenement called *Palmereshulle* formerly held by John le Palmere. Another source in 1372 records meadows bearing names such as *la Hame* (*le Home* 1340), *Ceveley* or *Geveley*, and *Loghesmed'*; in 1381 we have *Mortimersmote, Lokedemerschere', Forestfeld* and *Brodemede* and in 1454 we find *Le Laund, Revesmedowe* and *Lordesorchard* and the names of mills.[7]

There is also evidence of English settlement in purely rural areas, particularly in English Talgarth and Cantref Selyf between Brecon and Hay. Rees[8] mentions *Finchley* and *Kendershall* in English Talgarth to which we can add Trewalkin; in Cantref Selyf we find Tregunter, Tredyrn, Trehendre, Trephilip, Trebois (Boiston) and Tredwstan which – despite their Welsh appearance – mask English place-names. Nearer to Brecon there is Alexanderstone. These place-names are important not simply because they indicate English immigration but because the great majority also became cymricised at a later date. Very little is known of those who gave their personal-names to these places though Trephilip was reputedly 'built by Philip ap John Lawrence Bullen' and the lords of Trebois (Boiston) were said to be descended from Sir Richard Bois[9] but there seems to be no confirmation in other historical sources.

---

[6]  GRO D/D CL man/box 3: extent of Hay printed by R. Morgan (author) as 'An Extent of the Lordship of Hay' in *Brycheiniog* 28, pp. 15-21.

[7]  PRO SC.6/1156/18; Staffordshire Record Office D.641/1/2/246; GRO D/D CL man/box 3.

[8]  William Rees, pp.207-8

[9]  Poole, pp.180,181

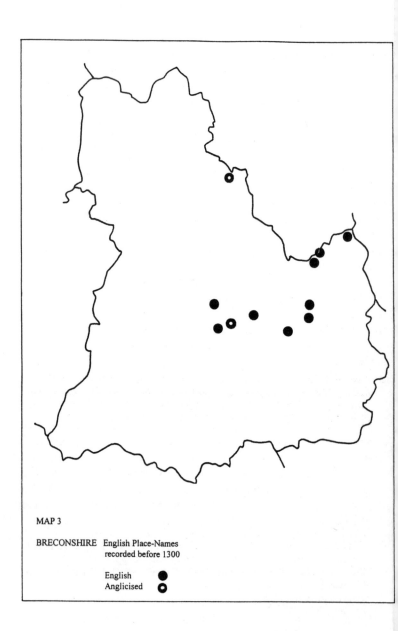

MAP 3

BRECONSHIRE   English Place-Names
recorded before 1300

English        ●
Anglicised     ○

In the period between c.1400 and c.1650 what evidence there is suggests that the English element in the local population was assimilated and that the English language was largely replaced by Welsh. In Brecon in 1542 only 30 out of 192 taxpayers bore English names.[10] The language which the taxpayers used is not, of course, specified but it may nonetheless be taken as evidence of increasing Welsh influence and of an increased use of Welsh. This supposition is partly borne out by Hugh Thomas's remarks in 1698 that of 400 families in the borough and parish 'there are now scarce thirty of English Name and Descent'.[11] Many in Brecon were bilingual: when George Fox and his companions visited it in 1657 his inn was full of people speaking Welsh but they switched to English at his request and 'had great discourse'.[12]

Welsh probably reached its maximum limit in Breconshire in the 17thC but it is very difficult to be certain. Our evidence increases in the 18thC. W.T.R. Pryce has compiled a map to show the geographical distribution of the English and Welsh languages c.1750 based upon the Visitation Returns, i.e. the evidence of the languages used in Anglican churches.[13] In about two-thirds of Breconshire the preferred language was Welsh and 'English-only' was confined to the area around Hay but there was an intervening area – broad between Hay, Brecon and Crucywel – where the church services were held in both

[10] R.R. Davies, 'Brecon', p.68; v. also William Rees, esp. pp.216-7 and Siôn Cent's poem 'i Frycheiniog': *Cywyddau Iolo Goch ac Eraill*, ed. H. Lewis, T. Roberts and I. Williams (Cardiff 1937), pp.268-9, referring to the 'profoundly Welsh character of the lordship of Brecon' in the 15thC: Llinos Beverley Smith, 'The Welsh language before 1536' in *The Welsh Language before the Industrial Revolution*, p.32.

[11] Hugh Thomas, *Towards a seventeenth-century History of Brecknock* (reprint Brecon 1967)

[12] Rev. T. Mardy Rees, *A History of the Quakers in Wales* (Carmarthen 1925), p.40.

[13] Geraint H. Jenkins, *The Foundations of Modern Wales 1642-1780* (Oxford 1987), p.398; v. also G.J. Lewis, 'The Geography of Cultural Transition: The Welsh Borderland 1750-1850', *The National Library of Wales Journal* 21 (1980), p.134, and refs.

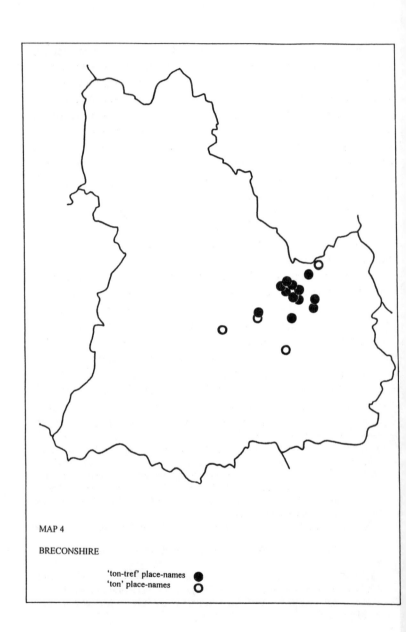

MAP 4

BRECONSHIRE

'ton-tref' place-names ●
'ton' place-names ○

14

languages. About the same period roughly one-third of Montgomeryshire and a half of Radnorshire were already 'English-only'.

The progress of anglicisation can be traced in the maps compiled by G.J. Lewis for c.1750, c.1800 and c.1850. Between 1750 and the early 19thC English made little progress beyond Hay and its vicinity: the area of Welsh-and-English services barely changed. At that time English was mainly confined to the towns of Brecon, Builth, Hay and Crucywel.[14] This was the same area where the early English Methodist chapels were established: at Brecon c. 1750 and Hay 1771, but few of the people in Talgarth at least knew English since Howel Harris had to translate the words of a visiting preacher for them.[15] The first Welsh Wesleyan chapel appeared at Llangynidr in 1808.

Anglicisation spread to the Crucywel area during the early 19thC. Archdeacon Payne says that in 1806 most of the rural parishes here adjoining Monmouthshire were predominantly Welsh speaking though he adds that the language in Llanbedr Ystrad Yw was 'much adulterated' by English.[16] It remains unclear what proportion of the population was bilingual. According to Payne the common people held not only to the Welsh language but to customs such as *gwyl mabsant*, distinctive Welsh dress and folk-lore.[17] In 1839 fluency in Welsh was still regarded as an essential prerequisite for a rector of Llanfeugan by Colonel Tynte, the holder of the living[18], which

---

[14] A.J. Ellis, 'On the Delimitation of the English and Welsh Languages', *Y Cymmrodor* 5 (1882), p.204.

[15] David Young, *The Origin and History of Methodism in Wales and the Borders* (London 1893), pp. 135, 149; G.F. Nuttall, *Howel Harris 1714-1773* (1965), p.34.

[16] David Young., p.142

[17] Powys County Archives Office Brecknock Museum A. 104/1/1 (1), pp.15, 133-9. Their beliefs included witches, the Tylwyth Teg y Coed and Bendith y Mamau; the last is also recorded in Monmouthshire: v. Edmund Jones, *The Geographical, Historical and Religious Account of Aberystruth* (1779).

[18] GRO D/D CL deeds ii. BRE 7997: letter from C.C. Clifton, Tŷ Mawr, Llanfrynach, to Thomas Mullins of Goathurst, Somerset, regarding the resignation of Leyson Penoyres from the rectory, the willingness of Tynte to

suggests that there was a significant number of people unable to speak English with any fluency; other sources over the following period record the progress of English. English was 'gaining ground fast' at Talgarth in 1848 and was said to be understood by all 'with the exception of a few old people'.[19] At Trefeca the position was similar and the local dialect was reckoned 'an admixture of Welsh and English'.[20] This same situation prevailed in Llanelli and ajoining parts of Monmouthshire[21]; by 1886 there were Welsh chapels only at Aber, Bryn-mawr (Bethesda), Dyffryn Crawnon, and Beaufort (Carmel) – the last just inside Monmouthshire – and at Llanelli.[22] This represented only about a third of those chapels in the same area using Welsh eleven years earlier.[23] Plainly, chapels were switching from Welsh to English; we know, for example, that the Wesleyan chapels at Llan-faes, Defynnog, Pwllgloyw and Lock (SO 0727) transferred from a Welsh to an English circuit at this period.[24]

By 1882 large parts of Breconshire were bilingual – the next step in many parts of Wales before complete loss of Welsh – and Crucywel was predominantly English speaking.[25] Ten years later Welsh was 'nearly extinct' in Cwmiou and the adjoining area called Y Ffwddog (formerly a detached part of Herefordshire, later part of Monmouthshire) and Southall was told that there was 'a host' of people able to speak Welsh twelve

---

present Clifton's son to the living, and the postponement of the necessary conveyance until the son attained fluency in Welsh.

[19] Rev. Morgan in *Reports of the Commissioners of Inquiry into the State of Education in Wales*. (London 1848), p.352.

[20] Rev. David Charles, Principal of Treveca, *ibid.*, p.354.

[21] *ibid.*, p.357, pp.399-411.

[22] Poole, p.362.

[23] *Worrall's Directory of South Wales and Newport*, pp.57-58 records Bryn-mawr (Baptist, Wesleyan and Calvinistic Methodist), Llanelli (Baptist, Independent), Darrenfelen (Wesleyan, Independent), Gilwern (Independent); 144: Crucywel (Methodist, Baptist), Llangynidr (Baptist), Tre-twr and Cwm-y-rhos near Cwm-du (Independent).

[24] David Young, p.149.

[25] Ellis, p.204.

years earlier including some of the children.[26]

Industrialisation evidently played a part in the decline of Welsh in the industrial parts of Breconshire at this period. Industry brought immigrants, particularly to 'the Numerous Iron Works . . . in the Mountains', i.e. around Bryn-mawr.[27] Industrialisation was not, however, a factor in rural northern and eastern Breconshire where there is also evidence of anglicisation in this period. In Brecon, English was 'gaining ground' in 1847 though still not universally spoken according to the Revd J. Denning, curate of St Mary's (whose attitude towards Welsh was remarkably bigoted even by the standards prevalent among Anglican clergy of that time).[28] By 1882 we know that chapels at Brechfa (Llandyfalle), Tal-y-bont, Talgarth, Glasbury, Tredwstan, Hay and perhaps Llangynidr were 'English only', and that English was gaining ground at Llangatwg and Pennorth.[29]

Further north English had made considerable progress in the immediate vicinity of Builth in that area adjoining the river Wye and Radnorshire in the period before 1882. The Religious Census 1851 indicates that most of the Anglican churches there south and west of Builth still had Welsh services[30] but by 1882 a correspondent of A.J. Ellis recorded only a 'little Welsh' in the neighbourhood of Builth and described Gwenddwr and Llangynog as bilingual. Builth church still had its Welsh bible but the vicar remarked that 'it does not seem to have been used within the recollection of any living person'.[31] Anglicisation

---

[26]  John E. Southall, *Wales and her Language* (2nd ed. London 1893), pp.348, 353: 'Yr oedd bacat yn siarad Cymraeg deugain mlynedd yn ôl a rhai o'r plant'.

[27]  Payne, p.133. Locals still preferred Welsh and were suspicious of strangers. See also Siân Rhiannon Williams, 'The Welsh Language in Industrial Monmouthshire, *c.* 1800-1901', *Language and Community* . . . (cited above).

[28]  Reports I, p.359. To Denning 'getting rid of the Welsh language' was necessary and knowledge of English would produce 'a healthy tone' in society, driving away the 'bigotry of the preachers', i.e. the Nonconformists.

[29]  Poole, p.362.

[30]  *The Religious Census of 1851. A Calendar of the Returns Relating to Wales*, ed. Ieuan Gwynedd Jones and David Williams (Cardiff 1976), I, pp.562, 565.

[31]  Ellis, p.203.

was not confined to Anglican churches. Poole records English chapels at Crucadarn, Gwenddwr, Llanwrthwl and perhaps Cefn-y-bedd; the services at Olewydd Congregational chapel, Llanwrthwl, established in 1847, too were mainly English.[32]

Tracing the history of Welsh and English in Breconshire is a difficult task but attempting to *explain* changes in their relative distribution is even more difficult. The reasons for the decline of languages have been studied extensively by others and it has been proposed that languages spread in three ways, i.e. by (1) 'expansion diffusion' (2) 'relocation diffusion' and (3) 'hierarchical diffusion'. The proposals are not meant, of course, to be taken in isolation from each other. When we apply these proposals to the available evidence it is perhaps unsurprising to discover that the precise reasons for the decline of Welsh or English in Breconshire at a particular date remain elusive and are likely to remain so: what makes clear theoretical sense is let down by the nature of the evidence. By contrast, it is relatively simple to describe the way and the pattern in which a language declines in comparison with any attempt at explaining that pattern: why, for example, was Welsh in retreat in the Builth area at an earlier date (late 18thC) than Crucywel (mid-19thC)?

'Expansion diffusion' demands social and commercial contact: Welsh declined when Welsh speakers adopted the English spoken by neighbours, friends and commercial colleagues. In Breconshire, Welsh-speakers who regularly attended meetings and markets in towns such as Hay and Brecon (and indeed Hereford) might be expected to have become bilingual. 'Relocation diffusion' is migration. The immigration of English speakers from Ireland, England and elsewhere undoubtedly had a marked effect in the industrial areas of Breconshire: immigrants required services, commercial and spiritual, in their own language. Small numbers of immigrants could be easily absorbed but large numbers of English-speaking immigrants, particularly evident in industrial

---

[32] *Congregational Year Book 1933.*

areas, made absorption very unlikely particularly in the case of Irish immigrants whose religion set them aside from the Nonconformist chapel and Anglican church. 'Hierarchical diffusion' was the process which took place when the gentry and industrialists had abandoned their Welsh (if they had ever possessed it – some after all were English immigrants); their adopted language would then pass down the social scale. Those in closest contact with them would be the first to become bilingual: the agent of an estate, the squire's housekeeper, the manager of a coal-mine, the foreman of an ironworks. If we couple these elements with the tremendous pressure of a state which paid little regard for Welsh and which had little use for it in administration and courts of law, and an established church and schools – particularly Church schools and endowed grammar schools – which frequently regarded Welsh as a barrier to 'progress' and a squirearchy that increasingly came to regard English as the language of 'polite society', then it is not difficult to understand why Welsh-speaking declined.

Topography has been seen as crucial with valleys providing routeways that were 'vulnerable to language shifts', in other words 'expansion diffusion.'[33] Roads used by long-distance travellers demanded post-houses, hostelries and smithies serviced by people able to speak English. Jenkins, Suggett and White have identified *inter alia* the valleys of the Severn, Wye and Usk as 'gateways for the English tongue' but the Wye above Llys-wen and the Usk above Abergavenny were not particularly important in this respect until the middle of the 19thC. The evidence rather suggests that English in Breconshire spread east to west from Radnorshire towards Builth in the late 18thC and from Hay southwestwards towards Brecon and Crucywel in the early 19thC. Anglicisation around Builth may well have been encouraged by the growing popularity of the line of spas stretching from Llandegle and Llandrindod in Radnorshire to Builth, Llangamarch and Llanwrtyd. In central

---

[33] Jenkins, Suggett and White in *The Welsh Language* . . . p.57.

and eastern Breconshire Welsh survived a little longer in the area immediately south-west of Crucywel and around Gwenddwr, Erwood and the eastern slopes of Mynydd Epynt.

Market-towns and commercial contacts were important contributors to this process. We have already noted the bilingualism of Brecon in the 17thC and 18thC, a bilingualism demanded not simply by trade but by the regular meetings of the magistrates in Quarter Sessions and the meetings of Great Sessions. The formal business of these courts was conducted in English (Latin was abandoned for formal records in 1733) though Welsh still dominated the countryside immediately outside the county town: in 1804, for example, a churchwarden of Battle complained that most of the parishioners stayed away from church because so much English was used in the services.[34]

---

[34]   *The Welsh Language* . . . , p.246.

# Breconshire's Place-Names

What has already been said in *A Study of Radnorshire Place-Names* (Welsh Heritage Series No. 7. Gwasg Carreg Gwalch, 1998) can be applied generally to Breconshire but there are some important differences with regard to the distribution of English place-names which themselves point to differences in the history of Welsh and English in the former county. These are summarised above under 'The Welsh Language in Breconshire'.

Our list below contains 340 separate entries and it cannot be regarded as anything other than a small, arguably unrepresentative, sample of Breconshire's place-names. Fairer analysis would demand a comprehensive collection of all place-names, hill-names and river-names drawn perhaps from the OS 1:10,000 plans with the addition of 'lost' place-names and all identified spellings taken from historic sources. That is clearly beyond the brief here but we shall be satisfied if it encourages others to study Breconshire's place-names in more depth. What follows is essentially a list of names of towns, parishes, hamlets, older geographic divisions such as hundreds and commotes, and a small number of hill-names.

Any arguments that rest on this small sample – and, of course, any conclusions that we reach – have to to be treated with caution; no doubt, further research will question our findings as more historic spellings are discovered. The list too – like that in *A Study of Radnorshire Place-Names* – is composite since it includes both names of great antiquity such as Usk/Wysg, Brecknock/Brycheiniog and Mynydd Epynt, and names of very recent origin such as Halfway, Beaufort and Libanus. The importance of recognising this has to be borne in mind in reading this book: place-names have both a geographic and an historic dimension and it would be a distortion if we ignored one for the other. As an example, if we were to plot on a map of Breconshire all known major English place-names, ancient and modern, it would give a very misleading impression since the distribution of these (and by implication the English language) varies according to a particular historical period.

If we compare Breconshire with Radnorshire (in *A Study of Radnorshire Place-Names*) we can appreciate the differences between them both in regard to the history of the English and Welsh languages and in regard to the place-names left by them. Radnorshire possessed at least twelve English place-names (excluding river-names) and one hybrid place-name (Glasbury) for the period before 1100 whereas Breconshire had only one. Breconshire also has only one mention of a place-name in Domesday Book 1086 and that itself is essentially nominal and *Welsh* (for *Calcebuef*, see Builth below). For the period before 1200 Radnorshire has at least fourteen English place-names compared with only three in Breconshire, viz. Hay, Pipton and Weynard's Castle (lost), and arguably four if we include Brecon (see Map 2). Latinised spellings such as *Breconia* applied to the castle and town, as administrative centre of Brycheiniog, suggest that it was already gaining a distinctive anglicised name in Anglo-French records which eventually became fixed as *Brecon*. No doubt our statistics in regard to both counties could be significantly amended if we possessed more early historic sources but they probably serve as a rough guide to the different balance of place-names in Radnorshire and Breconshire. Some places recorded in later sources are very likely to be 'early' in both cases, eg. Trewalkin (which appears as *villam Walkelini*) and Mara (see Llyn Syfaddan) which occur in early 13thC sources.

The contrast between Radnorshire and Breconshire remains sharp throughout the greater part of their history. By 1300 we can only add Newton (Llan-faes), Battle (a transferred name), Alexanderstone and Builth (an anglicised place-name like Brecon) to our English place-names for Breconshire, a total of only 3% of the place-names in our list of 340 entries below (see

Map 3). Despite this figure, there is some evidence that English had made a more marked impression on some parts of Breconshire. There is evidence of a considerable number of minor English names in and around Brecon and Hay (mentioned above in 'The Welsh Language in Breconshire') and there is a particularly interesting group of English place-names in the area between these towns (see Map 4). We might loosely term these 'ton-tref doublets': none of these is obviously English at first sight since they have Welsh *tref*, 'farm, township' (later 'town'), as their first element. If we look at older spellings, however, we find that, in English circles at least, they have ME *ton*, almost certainly with the same sense as *tref*, combined with a non–Welsh personal-name:

Trebois (*Boys-*, *Boiston* 1380): probably the F locative pers.n. *Bois* or *de Bois*.
Tredurn (*Duynour-*, *Dynourton* 1380): possibly a pers.n. derived from *Dinedor* HER.
Tredwstan (*Dorstonstone* 1303): probably AF *Turstan*, *Thurstan*.
Tregunter (*Gunterston* 1380): F *Gontier*.
Trehendre (*Hieston* for *Harieston* 1380): AF *Henri*, *Henry*.
Trephilip (*Phelippes-*, *Phillipeston* 1380): AF *Philip*.
Trewalkin (cited above): AF *Walchelin*.
Trewalter (*Walterstone Goch* c.1322-3): F *Gautier*, E *Walter*.

Trefeca may also belong to this group (see below) together with Trefithel (*Ytheleston* 1380), Troed-yr-harn (Tredrahaearn) (*Traharneston* 1372) near Brecon and an identical pn. (*Traharneston* 1331) at Talgarth, though their pers.ns. appear to be W *Ithel* and *Trahaearn*. All twelve place-names had become cymricised before 1500. Their identification is important since they increase the number of English medieval place-names in Breconshire to at least nineteen, a minimum of 5.2% of the place-names in our list. They are doubly interesting since their English names were apparently lost, in nearly all cases, before

1500: a sign we can suppose of a decline in the number of English speakers in the county.

## Explanation of the entries

A full explanation of the criteria used in selecting the place-names for analysis is set out in *A Study of Radnorshire Place-Names* (Welsh Heritage Series No.7. Gwasg Carreg Gwalch 1998). Briefly, we have assumed that the reader is not a specialist in place-name study and that the reader is not familiar with the history and geography of Breconshire. Specialists in place-name studies will recognise the ways in which this list differs from the academic's method of analysing place-names. In particular we omit source references and have limited the discussion of individual place-names. Essentially, this study is intended for the general reader and the local historian but we hope that students of language and place-name scholars will find it interesting. From our knowledge of the former county we feel sure that a great deal of what is set out below will be new to many people interested in Breconshire and the general subject of place-names.

The area of study is the old county of Breconshire as it existed in the period 1889 to 1974 together with the area around Trefil which was added to the old Ebbw Vale Rural Sanitary Authority MON in 1878. Most of Breconshire became a single borough within the new county of Powys in 1974. Our area thus includes Faenor (transferred to Mid Glamorgan in 1974 and Merthyr Tydfil County Borough in 1996) and Penderyn (transferred to Mid Glamorgan in 1974 and Rhondda Cynon Taff County Borough in 1996) together with Bryn-mawr and Llanelli (transferred to Gwent in 1974 and Blaenau Gwent County Borough in 1996). Breconshire lost its borough status and became part of the unitary authority of Powys in 1996.

Each entry follows a set format:

(a) The name in bold letters according to its authentic spelling –

not necessarily that of the OS. Generally speaking, if a place has an English name, such as Three Cocks and Sennybridge, this takes precedent over the Welsh name in the alphabetical order of the entries. The Welsh form in such cases is shown immediately after the 'lead form'. When a place has only a Welsh name we have preferred to employ the standard Welsh spelling, e.g. *Crucywel* (not *Crickhowell*) and *Llanelli* (not *Llanelly*).

(b) The four-figure OS grid reference, except in the case of those names applying to rivers and wide territorial units.

(c) A small selection of place-name spellings with dates of occurrence. Dates given refer to the actual date given in the original manuscript or source, not the date of the manuscript which may have been copied up later. We have added dates of manuscripts only when they were compiled *many* years afterwards. As an example, one source the Black Book of St. David's 1516 includes a survey compiled in 1326; our study records the date of spellings in the survey as 1326 (1516).

(d) A short discussion of each place-name. We have attempted to keep this as brief as possible and to avoid scholarly terminology. When we have used terms such as *epenthesis* and *provection*, we have added an explanation. Many readers will also know that the meaning of many place-names is obscure and that the explanation of their development is sometimes difficult and for these reasons will readily understand the somewhat tedious caution and the repetitive 'possibly' and 'probably'. We have not given lengthy references to academic publications and the sources of the spellings but a record of these has been kept by Richard Morgan in case anyone wishes to consult them.

The choice of which entries to include and which to exclude was difficult but we follow the format set out in *A Study of Radnorshire Place-Names*, ie. to include all those names shown on the OS 1:250,000 map covering Breconshire published in 1989, to which we have added the names of ancient *cantrefi*, hundreds, commotes, manors and reputed manors, ecclesiastical parishes and chapelries, townships, many hamlets and the main rivers. In some cases, we have combined the discussion of separate place-names under a single entry and cross-referred, e.g. Brycheiniog see Brecon.

## Abbreviations

| | |
|---|---|
| ADG | G.O. Pierce, T. Roberts a H.W. Owen, *Ar Draws Gwlad* (Gwasg Carreg Gwalch, Llanrwst 1997) |
| adj. | adjective |
| AF | Anglo-French |
| ANG | Anglesey |
| BRE | Breconshire |
| Brit | British, Brittonic |
| Brych | *Brycheiniog* (The Brecknock Society and Museum Friends 1955.) |
| chp(s). | chapel(s) |
| CNW | Cornwall |
| CRD | Cardiganshire |
| CRM | Carmarthenshire |
| CRN | Caernarfonshire |
| CVPN | Deric John, *Cynon Valley Place-Names* (Gwasg Carreg Gwalch 1998) |
| def.art. | definite article |
| DEPN | Eilert Ekwall, *The Concise Oxford Dictionary of English Place-Names* (Oxford 4th edition, 1960) |
| DES | P.H. Reaney and R.M. Wilson, *A Dictionary of English Surnames* (London 1991) |
| DNB | Denbighshire |
| E | English |
| EANC | R.J. Thomas, *Enwau Afonydd a Nentydd Cymru* (Cardiff 1938) |
| el(s). | element,-s |

| | |
|---|---|
| EPNE | A.H. Smith, *English Place-Name Elements* (EPNS, Cambridge 1956) |
| EPNS | The English Place-Name Society |
| ETG | Melville Richards, *Enwau Tir a Gwlad*, gol. Bedwyr Lewis Jones (Caernarfon 1998) |
| EWGT | *Early Welsh Genealogical Tracts*, ed. P.C. Bartrum (Cardiff 1966) |
| F | French |
| FLI | Flintshire |
| fem. | feminine |
| GLA | Glamorgan |
| GM | *Y Geiriadur Mawr*, gol. H. Meurig Evans a W.O. Thomas (Llandybïe 1978) |
| GPC | *Geiriadur Prifysgol Cymru*, (Caerdydd 1950-) |
| Haslam | see Bibliography |
| HER | Herefordshire |
| Ir | Irish |
| LCNC | *Language and Community in the Nineteenth Century*, ed. Geraint H. Jenkins (Cardiff 1998) |
| Leland | *Itinerary in Wales of John Leland, in or about the years 1536-9*, ed. Lucy Toulmin-Smith (London 1906) |
| lp(s). | lordship,-s |
| masc. | masculine |
| ME | Middle English (c.1150-c.1500) |
| ModE | Modern English (c.1500 to present) |
| ModW | Modern Welsh |
| MON | Monmouthshire |
| MTG | Montgomeryshire |
| MW | Middle Welsh |
| n(s). | name,-s, noun,-s |
| NCPN | B.G. Charles, *Non-Celtic Place-Names in Wales* (Cardiff 1938) |
| OE | Old English (c.400-c.1150) |
| OED | *The Oxford English Dictionary*, ed. J.A. Simpson and E.S.C. Weiner (2nd edition, Oxford 1989) |

| | |
|---|---|
| OF | Old French |
| OG | Old German |
| OIr | Old Irish |
| OS | Ordnance Survey |
| OScand | Old Scandinavian |
| OW | Old Welsh |
| p(s) | parish(es) |
| Parochialia | see Bibliography |
| PEM | Pembrokeshire |
| pers.n(s). | personal-name,-s |
| pl. | plural |
| pn(s). | place-name,-s |
| PNANG | Gwilym T. Jones and Tomos Roberts, *The Place-Names of Anglesey* (Bangor 1996) |
| PNDEF | R.F. Peter Powell, *The Place-Names of Devynock Hundred* (Pen-pont, Brecon 1993) |
| PNDP | G.O. Pierce, *The Place-Names of Dinas Powys Hundred* [GLA] (Cardiff 1968) |
| PNEF | Hywel Wyn Owen, *The Place-Names of East Flintshire* (Cardiff 1994) |
| PNHER | Bruce Coplestone-Crow, *Herefordshire Place-Names* (BAR British Series 214, 1989) |
| PNPEM | B.G. Charles, *The Place-Names of Pembrokeshire* (Aberystwyth 1992) |
| pron. | pronounced, pronunciation |
| r(s). | river,-s |
| RAD | Radnorshire |
| ref(s). | reference,-s |
| rn(s). | river-name,-s |
| sing. | singular |
| SHR | Shropshire |
| sp(s). | spelling,-s |
| SSX | Sussex |
| t(s). | township,-s |
| W | Welsh |

| WATU | Melville Richards, *Welsh Administrative and Territorial Units* (Cardiff 1973) |
| WLIR | *The Welsh Language before the Industrial Revolution*, ed. Geraint H. Jenkins (Cardiff 1997) |
| WOR | Worcestershire |

## Bibliography

The following list comprises those books and articles which we have found most useful in compiling this volume on Breconshire place-names and which we think are likely to prove of value to anyone interested in this subject, the history of Breconshire and the wider subject of Welsh place-names.

### Welsh History

Place-names have an historical background. Wales now has a new history appearing as volumes in a series. The following are most useful:

R.R. Davies, *Conquest, Co-existence and Change. Wales 1063-1415* (Oxford and Cardiff 1987)
Glanmor Williams, *Recovery, Re-orientation and Reformation. Wales c.1415-1642* (Oxford and Cardiff 1987)

**Note also:**

*A Bibliography of the History of Wales* (2nd ed., Cardiff 1962) and *Supplements* in the *Bulletin of the Board of Celtic Studies* vols. 20, 23, 25.
J.E. Lloyd, *a History of Wales from the Earliest Times to the Edwardian Conquest* (3rd ed., 1939)
*Llyfryddiaeth Llenyddiaeth Cymraeg*, ed. T. Parry and M. Morgan (Cardiff 1976) and Supplement in the *Bulletin of the Board of Celtic Studies*.
*The Oxford Companion to the Literature of Wales*, compiled and ed. Meic Stephens (Oxford and New York 1986)

## Welsh Place-Names and Language

B.G. Charles, NCPN

B.G. Charles, PNPEM

Rev. Ellis Davies, *Flintshire Place-Names* (Cardiff 1959)

Elwyn Davies (ed.), *A Gazetteer of Welsh Place-Names* (Cardiff 1957)

Geraint H. Jenkins (ed.), WLIR and LCNC

Deric John, CVPN

Bedwyr Lewis Jones, *Enwau* (Gwasg Carreg Gwalch, Capel Garmon 1991)

Gwilym T. Jones and Tomos Roberts, PNANG

Howard C. Jones, *Place-Names in Glamorgan* (Risca 1976)

Anthony Lias, *Place-Names of the Welsh Borderlands* (Ludlow 1991)

J. Lloyd-Jones, *Enwau Lleoedd Sir Gaernarfon* (Cardiff 1928)

Allen Mawer, *A Survey of the Place-Names of Wales* (1932-3)

Richard Morgan gyda G.G. Evans, *Enwau Lleoedd Buallt a Maesyfed* (Gwasg Carreg Gwalch, Capel Garmon 1993)

Richard Morgan, *Welsh Place-Names in Shropshire* (author, Cardiff 1997)

Rev. Thomas Morgan, *Handbook of the Origin of the Place-Names in Wales and Monmouthshire* (Merthyr Tydfil 1887). [This needs to be followed with great caution]

T.J. Morgan and Prys Morgan, *Welsh Surnames* (Cardiff 1985)

John Morris-Jones, *A Welsh Grammar* (Oxford 1913)

Graham Osborne and Graham Hobbs, *Place-Names of East Gwent* (Abergavenny 1998)

Hywel Wyn Owen, *Enwau Lleoedd Bro Dyfrdwy ac Alun* (Gwasg Carreg Gwalch, Capel Garmon, 1991)

Hywel Wyn Owen, PNEF

Hywel Wyn Owen, *A Pocket Guide. The Place-Names of Wales* (Cardiff 1998)

G.O. Pierce, T. Roberts a H.W. Owen, ADG

Melville Richards, ETG

Melville Richards, WATU

R.J. Thomas, EANC

Ifor Williams, *Enwau Lleoedd* (Liverpool 1969)
S.J. Williams, 'Some Breconshire place-names', Brych XI (1965)

## British and English Place-Names
Kenneth Cameron, *English Place-Names* (London 1961; 3rd edition 1977)
Bruce Coplestone-Crow, PNHER
John Field, *English Field Names. A Dictionary* (Gloucester 1989)
Eilert Ekwall, DEPN
Eilert Ekwall, *English River-Names* (Oxford 1928 and 1968)
Margaret Gelling, *Place-Names in the Landscape* (London 1984)
Margaret Gelling, *Signposts to the Past* (London 1988)
Margaret Gelling, W.F.H. Nicolaisen and Melville Richards, *The Names of Towns and Cities in Britain* (London 1970)
A.D. Mills, *Oxford Dictionary of English Place-Names* (2nd ed., Oxford 1998)
P.H. Reaney, *The Origins of English Place-Names* (London 1960)
Adrian Room, *A Dictionary of Place-Names in the British Isles* (London 1988)
Adrian Room, *A Concise Dictionary of Modern Place-Names in Britain and Ireland* (Oxford 1983)
A.H. Smith, EPNE

## Breconshire
*Atlas Brycheiniog* (Pwyllgor Addysg Brycheiniog, Aberhonddu 1960)
David Davies, *Hanes Plwyf Penderyn* (Aberdâr 1904)
Dewi Davies, *Brecknock Historian* (Brecon 1977)
Dewi Davies, *Welsh Place-Names of Breconshire and their Meanings* (Brecon 1971)
R. Davies, *Epynt without its People and much more* (1983)
Mrs. Gerard Finch Dawson, *The Churches of Breconshire* (Swansea 1909)
J.T. Evans, *The Church Plate of Breconshire* (Stow-on-the-Wold 1912)
T.O. Evans, *Roots & Branches* (Trecastell 1988)

G.L. Fairs, *A History of the Hay* (London and Chichester 1972)

Richard Haslam, *The Buildings of Wales. Powys* (Harmondsworth and Cardiff 1979)

Theophilus Jones, *A History of the County of Brecknock* [1805, 1809], ed. J.R. Bailey, Lord Glanusk (Brecon 1909-30)

D. Craionog Lewis, *Hanes Plwyf Crai* (Defynnog 1911)

D. Craionog Lewis, *Hanes Plwyf Defynnog* (Merthyr Tudful 1911)

John Lloyd, *The Great Forest of Brecknock* (London 1905)

Alun Llywelyn-Williams, *Crwydro Brycheiniog* (Llandybïe 1964)

Matthew Owen, *The Story of Breconshire* (Cardiff 1911)

Edwin Poole, *The Illustrated History and Biography of Brecknockshire* (Brecon 1886)

Edwin Poole, *The People's History of Brecon (Town and County)* (Brecon 1876)

E.H.V. Rees, *The Parish of Betws Penpont* (Brecon 1969)

*Hugh Thomas's Essay towards the History of Brecknockshire 1698*, ed. J. Jones Davies (Brecon 1967)

James Williams, *Brecon and its Neighbourhood* (Brecon no date)

# List and analysis of Breconshire Place-Names

**Aberbaidan** SO 2614
*aberbaydan* 1583, *ABERBAIDAN* 1804, *ABER BAIDON* 1811,
(house) *Aber-bidan* 1832

Identical to *Aberbaiden* GLA. W *aber* meaning 'mouth of a r.,
confluence', and the name of the r. *Baidan* or *Baedan* (*Baydan*
1583), probably containing W *baedd*, 'boar', with the suffix *-an*,
meaning a r. which rushes and darts like a wild pig.

**Aber-brân** SN 9829
*Aberbran* 1602, *Aberbraen* 1600-1, c.1765, *Aberbrayne* 1587,
*Aberbraine* 1568, *Aberbram* (= *-brain*) 1503; (grange of) *BRANE*,
*Bran'* 1326, (manor of) *Braan* 1379

W *aber* as in Aberbaidan with the rn. *Brân* (see Llanfihangel
Nant Brân below) meaning 'a crow', or figuratively, 'dark
river'. *Brân* was also a pers.n. but the late Bedwyr Lewis Jones
was inclined to doubt whether it is the element in rns. since it is
so common.

**Aber-craf, Abercrave** SN 8212
*Abercraf* 1690, *Abercrafe* 1832, *Abercrave House* 1798, *Abercraven*
1680

W *aber* and a rn. *Craf* (possibly now Nant Llech), probably W
*craf*, 'wild garlic', as in *Crafnant* (Dyffryn Conwy) CRN which
also has *nant*, generally 'stream'. The sps. with and the modern
pron. rhyming with E 'slave' may be attempts to represent local
dialect as in the case of *Aberdare* (*Aber-dâr* in standard W) GLA
which rhymes with E 'dare'. *Abercrave* was used for the house
built by the English industrialist Daniel Harper c.1798.

**Abercynrig**                                          SO 0727
*Aberconureg 1536-9, Aber Kynwric 1550, Aberconrik 1551, Aberkunfrig 1599, Abercundrick c.1745, Abercynrig 1832*

W *aber* and the rn. *Cynrig* 1832 (now no longer found on maps) which is thought to be the pers.n. *Cynwrig, Cynfrig*. It is interesting that some sps. have -*d*- as in the sp. of the modern surname *Kendrick* and *Gendros* GLA (from *Y Ge(f)nros*) and a similar feature (epenthesis) is found in E, eg. *thunder* < OE *thunor*. There is another *Abercynrig* in Crucadarn (SO 0739) which is *Aber Cynrig* 1832 and probably occurs in (house called) *Tyr Evan heare alias Aberkwnrig vechan* 1741; the r. here is now called *Nant y Mynach*, 'the monk's stream'.

**Aberduhonw**                                          SO 0650
*Haberdoneth, Ab(er)dehenowe 1535; Aberdohonwye c.1545, Aberde Hony 12thC (1425), ABERDIHANAW, Aberhoney Grange, Aberdehonoy 1202, Aberdehoney 1542, Aberdehonwy 14thC, Aberdihonw 1833*

W *aber* and a rn. *Duhonw(y)* but its meaning is obscure. The rn. may have the 'intensive prefix' as in *Dysynni* MER and *Digedi* BRE (the last reaches the Wye at SO 198411) which often precedes a noun: *Duhonw(y)* itself has -*wy*, -*w* and possibly the element found in *honni*, 'to assert, to pretend, to declare', but it is difficult to find any other examples of this in the sps. of other rns.

Duhonw was notable for its flooding. Murray's *Handbook for Travellers in South Wales* 1860 records that a flood in 1853 carried away 'a whole house' and 'a widow lady, with her children'. Aberduhonw was the site of a grange or farm belonging to the Cistercian monastery of Strata Florida.

**Abergwesyn**                                          SN 8552
*Abergwessyn* 1343-9, 1619; *aber gwesyn* c.1566, *Abergwessin* 1754

W *aber* and the rn. *Gwesyn* which is probably W *gwesyn* ( *gwas*, 'youth, young servant, page', with a suffix *-yn*). The rn. may have been used to distinguish the river as a tributary or 'servant' to its larger 'master', the r. Irfon.

**Aberllynfi: Three Cocks**                              SO 1737
*Abberlenevy* 1234, *Aberleneny* 1380, *Aberlun(vy)* 1305, *Aberleueni*, *-leweny* 1251, *Abrelleueny* 1536-9, *Aberllevenny* 1635, *Aberllynfi* 1778, *Abberlewin* [= *-lewni*], *Abrelenuith'* 1233
*Three Cocks* 1754, c.1817, (public house) *the Three Cocks* 1813, *Three Cocks Junc.* 1886

W *aber* and the rn. *Llynfi* which is *Lyfni* 12thC, *Leveni* 1176-98, *Leveny* 1331, *Lhynvi, Lhyfni* c.1700, *Llyfny* 17thC containing W *llyfn*, 'smooth, even', with the suffix *-i*, probably meaning 'smooth-flowing r.' There are similar rns. in CRN, GLA and DNB. The rn. is interesting because the *-n-* and the *-f-* (which has the sound of E *v*) have exchanged positions by a process called metathesis. There was formerly a chapel-of-ease (to Glasbury) that stood near Great House Farm which was said to have been destroyed by floods. Poole, a Breconshire historian, records in 1886 that the chp. fell into disuse in the 18thC and that there was a font dated 1635 at the entrance to the farm, later removed to Glasbury churchyard.

Aberllynfi now bears the alternative name *Three Cocks* which derives from the coat-of-arms of the Williams family of Gwernyfed (see below) and was adopted as the name of the hotel in the village. It has been claimed that Einion Sais, son of Bleddyn ap Maenarch, of Aberllynfi, bore the arms 'argent, three cocks gules', but these are late medieval inventions, though they are displayed at the former railway station. The inn name is found elsewhere in BRE; there was a dwelling-

35

house in the Struet, Brecon, 'formerly called the Three Cocks' 1758, later the 'Bull Inn', and a 'Three Cocks' in Talgarth 1859.

### Aberonneu    SO 2117
*Aberonny 1720, 1752; Blayne onney 1516,* (land) *Pen y Cwm Onney 1518-29, Cwm-onneu, Blaen Onneu,* (hill) *Cefn Onneu 1832*

W *aber* and the rn. *Onneu.* The sps. are very late but it would appear to be identical to the r. Onny SHR containing W *onn,* 'ash-trees'. Probably 'r. near which ash-trees grow'. The hamlet here is called *New Inn* and *Dafarn Newydd 1831-33* which mean the same.

### Aberysgir    SO 0029
*Aberescir c.1143-54, Abereschir c.1190-1200, Abereskyr early 13thC, Aber Ysgyr 15thC, ABRYSKER 1535, Abereskeire 1513, Abskerr 1380*

W *aber* and the rn. *Ysgir* which is *Eskir, Heskir c.1143-54, Eskir 1754, Ischir 11thC, Ysker 1602* containing W *ysgyr;* this could be an older pl. of *ysgwr,* 'branch, staff, piece of wood', according to S.J. Williams. Some sps. show that the rn. was confused with *esgair,* 'ridge'. Aberysgir also occurs as (church of) *Sancti Kenedri de ABERESKIR 1490* and *plwy Mair a chynnyd yn aberysgir c.1562,* the first meaning 'church of St. Cynidr' and the second meaning 'p. of Mary and Cynidr'. The original dedication of the church was probably to St. Cynidr, the same saint in Llangynidr, to which Mary (Mair) was added later, perhaps in the 13thC when her cult became popular. Well-known saints such as Mary were often added to existing dedications to local saints. *Cynidr* seems to have lost its unstressed *-r* in local speech, a common feature in spoken Welsh, just as *ffenestr,* 'window', is usually pronounced *ffenest.* The r. also gave its name to two hamlets in Merthyr Cynog named as *YSKIR-FAWR, ~ -FECHAN 1804,* 'big Ysgir' and 'little Ysgir'.

**Alexanderstone** SO 0730

*Alisandreston* 1373, *Alysaundrestoune* 1507, *Alsandreston* 1424, *Alexanderstone* 1483-4, 1595; *Alysaundres Towne* 1444, *Alexaunderstowne* 1508

'Alexander's farm or settlement'. The earliest sp. we have seen is that for 1373. We cannot find that 'Alexander' has been identified but the pers.n. is certainly found in Brycheiniog: William Alisaundre occurs c.1422-4 and William ap John Alisaunder was provost of the manor of Brecon 1453-4.

**Yr Allt** hill SN 9129

*Allt* 1832

'Slope, wooded slope'; the second meaning is general in south Wales.

**Allt Ddu** hill SO 0223

*Rallt* 1814, *Rallt-ddu* 1832

'Dark wooded-slope', with *allt* and *du*; because *allt* is fem. *du* mutates to *ddu*.

**Alltmarchan**

*Alt Marchan* 1582; *Tyr Allt Marchan* 1608, (reputed manor of) *Alltmarchan* 1608

Probably W *allt*, 'wooded slope', and *marchan*, 'little horse', or a pers.n. *Marchan* with the same meaning. The sps. are, however, rather late and it is possible that this may be the same place as *Carthmarthan* 1380 which seems to have been in the Llys-wen/Llandyfalle area and we know that Alltmarchan was a manor in Llandyfalle. *Carthmarthan* may well stand for *Garthmarchan* because initial G and C and *t* and *c* are sometimes confused in medieval script. If so, *allt* could have displaced W *garth*, 'hill, ridge'; alternatively, *Alltmarchan* and *Garthmarchan* are distinct ns. for adjoining places.

**Allt-mawr** SO 0746
*gallt-mawr* c.1566; *Alltmawr* 1615, *Altemawre* 1578, *Capel Allt-mawr* 1832

W *allt* (as above) and *mawr*, 'big, great', but our sps. are late and *allt* is generally fem.; in other words we would expect *Allt-fawr* with the adj. mutating. This was a chapel-of-ease to Llanafan Fawr and the dedication is said to have been to a certain *Mauritius* but this may be a fiction inspired by *-mawr*.

**Battle: Y Batel** SO 0031
(church) *de Bello* 1222-4, *Battle* 1527, 1689, *the Battell* 1598-9, *Battell* 1578, *Capely-Battel* 1754, *y battel* c.1566, (fms.) *Battle-fawr*, ~ *-fach*, ~ *-end* 1832

Named after *Battle* abbey SSX which held the advowson of the church. Battle abbey itself commemorated the Battle of Hastings 1066. Popular tradition associates our Battle with the battle in which Bernard de Neufmarché slew Rhys ap Tewdwr and Bleddyn ap Maenarch, the last of the W princes of Brycheiniog and Hugh Thomas records in 1698 a *Fynnon Pen Syr Rhees* (*Ffynnon Pen Syr Rhys*), two miles north of Battle, which may be translated 'well associated with Sir Rhys's head'. The W n. *Y Batel* can be compared with E 'battle' borrowed as W 'batel, batail, batl'. If *Syr Rhys* is a reliable sp., then it might refer to a clergyman since *Syr* was often used as a mark of respect like E *Reverend*.

**Beacons Reservoir** SN 9818

Named from the Brecon Beacons (below); one of several reservoirs, built by Cardiff Corporation in 1897.

**Beaufort: Cendl**                                        SO 1611
*Beaufort furnace 1794, Beaufort Furnace 1814, 1832, Beaufort Works
1798, Beaufort Arms Inn 1811, Kendle, Cendle 1839, Cendl 1867*

Beaufort began as a settlement next to the ironworks
established by Edward Kendall (originally from SHR), Jonathan
Kendall and Joseph Latham, under lease from the Duke of
Beaufort in 1779. The W n. *Cendl* derives from *Kendall* and
*Kendalls pitch* occurs near the town on the OS one-inch map in
1832. Edward Kendall (died 1807) became sheriff of Breconshire
and lived at Dan-y-parc near Crucywel. Beaufort had no less
than three inns called *the Beaufort Arms* in 1849. *Dukestown*
(*Dukes Town* 1832) MON is also named after the Duke of
Beaufort.
    Beaufort lay in the most southerly part of Llangatwg and
Llangynidr ps. but became a separate p. in 1846. In 1878 it was
added to Ebbw Vale Rural Sanitary Authority and passed to
MON in 1889. It now lies in Blaenau Gwent.

**Beulah: Beula**                                         SN 9251
*Beulah 1851, 1857*

Named from the Congregational chp. established here in 1821-2
and enlarged in 1841-2. A considerable number of villages in
Wales take their ns. from chps.; there is an interesting group of
such ns. (Soar, Hermon, Salem, Bethlehem) near Llandeilo Fawr
CRM. BRE also has Libanus below. In his vision the prophet
Isaiah says to the Forsaken that 'neither shalt thy land any more
be termed Desolate: but thou shalt be called Hephzi-bah, and
thy land Beulah' (Isaiah 62.4). The small settlement also
attracted the Anglicans: *Eglwys Oen Duw*, 'church of the lamb of
God', was built in 1865-7 by Miss Thomas of Llwynmadog.

**Black Mountain: Y Mynydd Du** hills
*ymynyd du 1217 (14thC), o'r Mynydd Du 15thC, Y Mynydh duy*

1584, *The black mountayne* 1578, *the Blake Montaine* 1536-9, *the Black Mountains in Caermarthenshire* 1814, *BLACK MOUNTAINS* 1798

W *mynydd* and *du* translated as 'Black Mountain'; 'black' in this case, as in many other upland BRE pns., probably refers to the dark aspect of north facing slopes. Some late E sources appear to confuse it with the Black Mountains (next). Probably the 'Black Mountain' recorded in a report sent to Edward II in 1316.

### Black Mountains: Mynydd y Gader
*Atterel Hylles . . . in Walsche Meneth e Cadair, id est montes alti instar cathedrarum* 1536-9; *Hatterills loftie hills, Black-Mountaine* 1612, *Hatterel hill* 1578, *HATTERALL HILL OR BLACK MOUNTAIN* 1816-17; *Mynyddy Gader* 1754, *the Gadair Mountains* 1806, *the Black Mountains of Talgarth* 1814, *y Mynydd-du* 1839

It is difficult to find early mentions of the *Black Mountains* and it is possible that the n. is an error and derives from John Leland, the antiquarian, who describes *Blak Montayne* as stretching from the vicinity of Monmouth to near Carmarthen, ie. incorporating the whole of the Black Mountains, Brecon Beacons and the Black Mountain above. Leland's other ref. (the first cited above) suggests that he regarded the Hatterall Hills as the same as Mynydd y Gader but the last may once have applied specifically to the hill now marked *Gader Fawr* and *Pen y Gader-fawr* (SO 229288); this has W *mynydd*, 'mountain', the def.art. *y* and *cadair, cader*, 'chair', ie. 'mountain shaped like a chair'. The best known example of this use of *cadair* is *Cader Idris* ('Idris's chair'), a mountain in MER. *Hatterall Hill* (SO 3025) is actually a distinct feature taking its n. from Hatterall HER.

### Blackrock                                      SO 2112
*Black rock in Llanelly* 1814, *Black-rock* 1832

The hamlet stands on the rocky edge of Cwm Clydach in

Llanelli p. and now lies in Blaenau Gwent. There was an inn here called the *Rock and Fountain* in 1849.

**Blaenau**                                                    SO 1926
Llanfihangel Cwm-du
*o'r Blaenau* 15thC, *Blaenau* 1832, *BLAENEY* 1804

**Blaenau**                                            SO 1212, 1217
Llangynidr
*Blainey* 1851

W *blaenau*, 'extremity, confines, uplands, headwaters', is the pl. of *blaen*, and is commonly applied to the upland part of a p. in contrast to its lowlands or *bro* (as in *Bro Morgannwg*, the lowland part or 'Vale' of Glamorgan). Llangynidr has a t. called *Fro* (see below). Just over the watershed from Llangynidr is *Blaenau Gwent*, the upland part of the old kingdom of Gwent. *Blaenau Ffestiniog* MER was the upland part of the p. of Ffestiniog.

**Blaendyryn**                                                SN 9336
*Blaen-derin* 1817; *Blaendyryn* 1839, *Cwm-r-deryn* 1832

W *blaen*, which is often used to mean the upper part of a valley where the main stream rises. *Dyryn* is the n. of a small stream here. The sps. are very late but it may have *aderyn, ederyn*, 'bird, young bird': 'river which dips and weaves like a bird'. The ns. of birds and animals are very common in W rns.

**Blaenllyfni, Blaenllynfi**                                   SO 1422
(castle) *Blanelleveni* 1233 (c.1286), *Blenleveny* 1230, 1322, *Blaynleveny* 1285, *Blaynllynuye* 1578, *Blaynllynvye* 1596-7, *blaenllyfni* 1215 (14thC), (borough) *Blaenllovenny* 1689, (castle., lp.) *Blenlevenyth* 1332, (church) *BLANEUENY* 1401

W *blaen* and the rn. *Llyfni* or *Llynfi*, for which see Aberllynfi (above). The church of Blaenllynfi recorded in 1401 and 1695 must be Cathedin below. John Leland, the antiquarian and scholar, 1536-9 mentions a 'very fair castel now dekeiyng'. In 1337 the towers of the castle are named as *Jeholestour, Turbervylestour, Pichardestour* and the *Nurse's Tower*. The Picard family were lords of the manor of Ystrad Yw which was a part of the lp. of Blaenllyfni; the Turbervilles were lords of Crucywel, but we cannot identify a family here with the surname *Jehole(s)* or *?Giles*. Perhaps it refers to Giles de Braose, a son of William de Braose, lord of Brecon. Giles is known to have captured Blaenllyfni castle in 1215 shortly before his death. Gileston, about two miles from Blaenllyfni castle may preserve the n. of some local family but it was certainly held for at least a part of its history by the Gunter family (see Gileston). It is very likely that these families – presumably with the exception of the Nurse's Tower, unless *Nurse* is really a surname also – were responsible for repairing and maintaining the towers. *Turbervylestour* is probably *Grimbaldestower* mentioned in 1433.

**Boiston** see **Trebois**

**Bolgoed**                                              SO 0027
*Bolgoyd* 1362, *bolgoit* 1522, *Bolgoid* 1536-9, *Bolgoed* 1689, 1702-3, *Bolgoed-ganol,* ~ *-isaf* 1832, *Bolgod* 1684

There is another *Bolgoed* on the OS map 1832 near Upper Chapel and a *Bolgoed* near Loughor GLA. W *bol, bola* means 'belly' and *Bellymoor* HER was earlier called *Bolgros* (with W *rhos,* 'moor') meaning the same. There are even two places called *Rhos-y-rhumen* in Llanuwchllyn MER and Llanllyfni CRN in which *rhumen* also means 'belly'. *Bolgoed* would mean either 'wood in a hollow' or, more likely in this case, 'wood on a prominent mound'.

**Nant Brân**
*Bran flu:* 1573-80; *Nant-bran* 1832

See Aber-brân above and Llanfihangel Nant Brân below; *flu:* is Latin *flumen*, 'river'.

**Brecknock: Brycheiniog**
**Brecon: Aberhonddu**                                    SO 0428
*Bricheniauc* 895 (c.1000), *Brecheinawc* 848 (c.1400), *bricheinauc* 12thC, *Brechyeniok, Brekhnok* 1241, *Brekenoc* 1204-14, *Brecknock* 1545-6, *Brecckenioc* 1216, *y urycheinya6c* 12thC, *Tir Brycheinauc* c.1102-5 (c.1250)
(burgage in) *Brechonia* 1233 (late 13thC), (church of) *Brechonia* 1254, *Brechon'* 1291, *Brekon'* 1517
*Aberodny* 1216 (late 13thC), *aber hotni* 15thC, *Aber hodni, ~ -ei* 1543-53, *Aberhotheni* c.1200, *aber hoddni* 15thC, *Aberhonddi, Aber Hondhi* c.1700, *Aberhodni B. Breknoke A.* 1573-80, *i Gaerhodni* 15thC

*Brycheiniog* means 'land of Brychan', a pers.n. with the suffix *-iog*, common in W pns., especially for ancient lps. and hundreds (W *cantrefi*), such as Cyfeiliog MTG, Pebidiog PEM and Rhufoniog DNB. Brychan is said to have ruled this area in the 5thC and is credited with an unbelievable number of children but the evidence occurs in manuscripts which are 600 years or more later. *Brycheiniog* is stressed on the *-ein-* but E speakers shifted the stress to the first syllable to produce *Brecknock. Brecknock* is now confined as a n. to the former county, *Brecon* to the town, but they both derive from *Brycheiniog*, largely because Brecon was the administrative centre of Brycheiniog as in the case of Builth in *Buellt. Brecon* probably arose from latinised sps. such as *Brechonia* and abbreviated sps. such as *Brecon'* in the same way as *Salopia* and *Salop* derive from OE *Scrobbesbyrig*, frenchified as *Salopesbury*, the ancient forms of *Shrewsbury*.

The W n. for the town has *aber* in its usual sense of 'mouth of a r., confluence' and the rn. *Honddu*, earlier *Hoddni*. This occurs as *hotni* 13thC, *hodni* 1240, *Hothenei* c.1100, *Hodeni*, *Hotheni* c.1143-54, *Hodney* 1562, *Honthy* 1578 and in *Dyffrynn Hothny* 1443, *Dyffrin Honddye* 1536-9. The meaning of the rn. is uncertain but it may contain W *hawdd*, 'easy, happy, pleasant', and -*ni* a suffix sometimes found in other rns. such as *Rhymni* GLA/MON. Edward Lhuyd, the scholar and scientist evidently did not find the r. very pleasant because he describes it c.1700 as 'an ugly torrent . . . which falls with much noise & violence into Uske, at the upper end of Brecknock towne'. The sps. with -*ddu* are very late and may show popular association with W *du*, 'black, dark'.

*Gaerhodni* has a mutation *G*- after the preposition *i*, 'to', for *Caerhodni*, a fanciful n. used by the poet Huw Cae Llwyd. His son Ieuan describes Brecon as 'Aber sy benna seren, Hyd nef, Aberhodni wen': 'Fair Aberhodni, the greatest star as far as Heaven'.

### Brecon Beacons: Bannau Brycheiniog

*o uann u6ch deni* 15thC, *Mynydd Bannwchdêni* (*which some call*) *Bann Arthur* (and) *Moel Arthur* 1592, *Monuchdenye hil* 1578, *Monuchdennie* 1548, *Manuchdenny Hill or Cader Arthur* 1720, *Managhdeny, Banney* 1602, *Arthur Cadahir* c.1570, *The Vann or Brecknock Beacons* 1754, *FFOREST FAWR, Beacons* 1832

John Leland 1536-9 distinguishes between *Artures Hille*, which is probably the modern Pen y Fan, and *Banne Brekeniauc* which are the Brecon Beacons. *Bannau Brycheiniog* has W *bannau*, pl. of *ban*, 'peak, summit', and *Pen y Fan* as the highest of the Beacons is 'top, highest of the peaks'. *Artures Hille* is also the same as *Kaer Arthur*, 'that is, the chair of Arthur' – presumably King Arthur of legend – mentioned by Gerald of Wales c.1191. *Kaer* is not likely to be W *caer*, 'fort', but an error for *cadair, cader*, 'chair' (as in the sp. *Arthur Cadahir* above) often applied to glaciated mountains with a shape thought to resemble a chair with its round back and arms. The E n. *Brecon Beacons* is probably a translation of *Bannau Brycheiniog* with *beacons* being used to mean simply 'mountains' rather than places at which fires were lit.

Some of the other ns. for the Brecon Beacons are very curious. John Ogilby, the first road-map maker, 1675, mentions a *Bullavan* here, clearly *Bwlch-ar-fan* 1832 (SO 031200), and today's Bwlch ar y Fan, 'pass on or near the summit'. Rice Lewis, the antiquarian, says in his Breviat of Glamorgan 1596-1600 that the r. Taf 'springeth out of a hill called bwlch y van'. The r. Taf Fechan actually rises on the south slope of Pen y Fan and Taf Fawr rises on Corn Du ('black horn or point') on the west side of Pen y Fan.

*Monuchdenye* and similar sps. are thought to derive from the first ref. above taken from a poem of Lewys Glyn Cothi (1447-89) and standing for ModW *o Fan uwch Deni*, 'from the Peak above Deni', or from *Mynydd Bannwchdêni* 1592. *Deni* has not been satisfactorily explained but the following theory is worth considering. The present Y Fenni-fach (see below), earlier *Benni* 11thC, is given as the birthplace (in De Situ Brecheniauc) 11thC and sojourn (Cognacio Brychan 13thC) of Brychan. Close by is the Roman fort Y Gaer, named incorrectly as *Bannium* by Theophilus Jones 1805 (and the OS map 1832). *Benni* is thought to have been occupied in the post-Roman and pre-Norman period and in view of its associations with Brychan was plainly a site of particular importance. Can *Deni* be a scribal error for *Benni*, an error perhaps perpetuated by later antiquarians and map makers? If so, we may actually have 'the Peak above Benni', where *Benni* acts as a focal point to distinguish this peak from others in the same way as *Brecon Beacons* uses Brecon as its distinguishing el.

**Bishop's Town** see **Tre'resgob**

**Bronllys** SO 1435

*Brendlais* c.1200, *Brendlos* c.1200 (16thC), *Brenleis* 1210-12, *Brenthles* 1299, *Brentles* c.1291, *Brenlez* 1380, *Broynlles* 1553, *hyd Vrwynllys, o ur6nllys* 15thC, *Brynllis* 1524, *Bruntlys* 1804, *Bronllys* 1832, *Bremles* 1241

Possibly 'court of Brwyn': a pers.n. *Brwyn*, perhaps identical to *brwyn*, 'rushes', and *llys*, 'court, palace, hall'. Phillimore explained the early sps. with *Bren-* as containing an Old Celtic *e* 'which in Welsh becomes regularly *wy*'. The dipthong *wy* was gradually reduced to *y*, the 'obscure' W vowel, to produce *Brynllys* and in very recent times this was confused with *bron*, 'breast' and 'hill-side, slope', etc. to produce the modern sp. *Brwyn* has been identified with *bruin o bricheinauc* who occurs in the 12thC and S.J. Williams suggested that the Anglo-Norman castle here was built on the site of his court. The pn. is unlikely to be *breinllys, breintlys* (*braint* + *llys*), 'royal court', or 'court of Braint', because of the lack of early sps. with *Breint-, Breynt-* etc.

**Bronydd** SO 2245

*Bronydd* 1828, 1833, *Bronith Chapel* 1851

The sps. are really too late to help though it appears to be W *bronnydd*, pl. of *bron*, 'breast' and 'hill-side, slope'.

**Bron-rhydd** SN 9051

*Bron Rhydd* 1820-1, *Bron-rhudd* 1833

Perhaps *bron* as in Bronnydd and *rhudd*, 'red, crimson', but there are other possibilities such as *rhydd*, 'free', and *(y)r hydd*, 'the stag'.

**Bryn** hill SO 0722

*Llanfeugan Bryn* 1832

**Bryn** hill SN 9055

*Llanafan Fawr Bryn* 1820-1, 1833

W *bryn*, 'hill, mount, rise'. There was another Bryn, a manor recorded as *Bryn* 1380, possibly Bryn-du, Bronllys.

**Bryncarthog**                                      SN 8951
*Bryn Carthog* 1820-1, *Bryn carthog* 1833

W *bryn* and *carthog*, an adj. formed from *carth*, which has several meanings including 'offscourings, sweepings, offal, excrement', as in *carthbwll*, 'cesspool'. It could mean 'hill used for dumping offal or dung'.

**Bryn Du** hill                                      SN 9342
Llangamarch *Bryn-du* 1832

'Black hill'.

**Bryn Garw** hill                                      SN8361
*Bryn garw* 1833

Probably 'rough (or steep) hill' with *bryn* and *garw*, 'rough, coarse' and 'steep, challenging'. There is a pool about a mile to the east called *Llyn Carw* apparently with W *carw*, 'stag', though the stream which flows from it is *Nant-y-garw* (for *Nant Garw* ?) 1833, ? 'rough stream'; *carw* may well be a product of popular re-interpretation.

**Bryn-mawr**                                      SO 1911
*Brin Maure* 1587, *Bryn-mawr* 1832, *Brynmawr* c.1814, *Great Brin Town* 1830-35

'Big hill'. An industrial town established around Bryn-mawr farm and the 'Prince of Wales' inn c.1800 on the moor called *Gwaun yr Helygen*, 'willow-tree moor'; this is *Waun r Ellygon* 1794, *Gwayn yr Helycen* 1801, *Gwaun-helygen* 1832.

**Buallt (Buellt)** see **Builth Wells**

## Buckland: Bychlyd                           SO 1321

*lech bychlyt* 12thC, (well under) *Boghlek* c.1234-5, ~ *Bochelet* c.1234, (forest of) *Bogheled* 1482, *Bighlyd* 1589-90, *Bughled* 1600-7, *Bughlyd, Bighled* 1595, *Bucklond* 1626, *Buckland House* 1798

For many years, during its occupancy by the British Legion, the hall was known as Crosfield House, but today it has reverted to *Buckland Hall. Mynydd Buckland* 1832 is now *Buckland Hill.* Probably W *bwch*, 'buck, he-goat, roe-buck', and *llyd*, an adj. usually added to a noun; it may mean 'area abounding with bucks'. The *-w-* of *bwch* changes to the 'obscure' vowel *y* by a process called 'vowel-affection' when it is combined with *llyd*. Professor J.E. Lloyd showed that the west gate of Tre-tŵr castle was called *Porth Bychlyd* (*Porth Boket* c.1230-40). The modern sp. *Buckland* is very deceiving and probably arose through association with E *buck*, very likely in the knowledge that it meant the same as *bwch*, and *-llyd* was mixed up with E *land*.

An alternative n. for Buckland is sometimes said to be *Gwaunygeifr*, 'the goats' moor', but this is a distinct place in Llan-y-wern parish.

## Builth Wells: Llanfair-ym-Muallt          SO 0451

(town of) *Beult* 1533-8, (rectory of) *Buelth* 1567, *Buelth upon Wy* 1536-9, *Built* 1671, *Lanveyr* 1254, *Lanueir in Buelth* 1280, *Thlanver* 1335-6, *Lamueyr Buelth* 1282 (late 13thC), *lan fair y myellt* c.1556, *llanvayre in buylte*, ~ *bwyllte* 1578, *Lhanuair in Buelht* 1584, *Llanfair Muallt* 1831

The p. is still known officially as *Llanfair in Builth*, properly *Llanfair-ym-Muallt* or 'church of St. Mary in Buallt'. *Builth* originated as an E attempt to pronounce or write *Buellt*, the older form of *Buallt*, the n. of the hundred (cantref) in which the town lies. *Buellt* or *Buallt* occurs as *buellt* c.1100-3, *Buellt* 1170 (c.1286), *Buelt* 1207, *Buelt, Bouel, Buelitia regio* 8thC (early 13thC), (land of) *Bueld* c.1200, *atta6 Vuellt* c.1258 (c.1400), *am Vuellt* c.1400, *tir Buellt* 15thC, *kantref byellt* c.1566, (castle of) *Bovent* 1290-2; *Calcebuef* 1086, and means 'cow pasture(s)' with W *bu, buw*, 'cow, bullock', (as in *buarth*, 'farmyard', and *beudy*, 'cowshed') and *gellt*, ModW *gwellt*, 'grass', etc. The sp. as *Buallt* is much later and may have arisen through false association with the very common *allt*, 'slope, wooded slope'. Similar pns. occur elsewhere, eg. *Gwern y Buellt* 1624-5 which was near Goetre MON and *Y Fuallt* (SO 191517) RAD. No doubt *Builth* replaced *Llanfair* in the same way as *Brecon* replaced *Aberhonddu* BRE and *Cardigan* replaced *Aberteifi* CRD as the official E descriptions for those towns because they were the administrative centres of their ancient lps. One of the most interesting mentions is *Calcebuef* in Domesday Book 1086 which has been identified hitherto with a number of other places. At that time it was held by a certain *Riset*, ie. Rhys ap Tewdwr, ruler of Deheubarth, on payment of £40 annually to the king of England. The *-buef* is almost certainly a scribal error for *-buelt*; Domesday Book has a curious joined form of *l* and *t*, very much like its form of *f*. The first part of *Calcebuef* could represent some sp. of *cantref* (see Cantref below) or a miswriting of either F *chastel* or Latin *castellum*, 'castle', through omitting the *-el*-sound (repeated in *–buelt*) and mixing up the other letters, ie. *Chastel* ~, *Castellum Buelt* > *\*C(h)astelbuelt*, *\*Cast(e)buelt*, *Calcebuef*. Domesday Book is notorious for its curious sps. of many W and E pns.

*Wells* was a fashionable addition to *Builth* in the 19thC in reference to its saline, chalybeate and sulphurous wells at *Park Wells* mentioned in 1804-13 and *Glannau Wells*; compare Llanwrtyd Wells and Llangamarch Wells below. *Glannau Wells* lay near the farm called *Felin y glanau* 1833 (W *melin*, 'mill'); *glanau* must be W *glannau*, pl. of *glan*, 'bank'.

**Bwlch**                                                          SO 1422
*Bwlch* 1720, *The Bulch Inn* 1794, *Bwlch'r allwys* 1832

W *bwlch*, 'pass, gap', between Buckland Hill and Cefn Moel, through which a Roman road and the A40 pass. There was a 'waste' called *Koyd ybulghe* here in 1561, meaning 'wood (or trees) at the pass'. It is difficult to explain the 1832 sp., taken from the OS 1 in. map; it certainly looks like an error.

**Bwlchefengyl: Gospel Pass**                                    SO 2335
*dyr uyncul* 12thC, *Bulchy Vingle* 1754, *Bwlch-y-Fingil* 1828, *Bwlch-y-fingel* 1832

Older sps. are scarce but the modern sps. may well be deceptive. The first el. is evidently W *bwlch* and the second el. would *appear* to be *efengyl*, 'gospel', as the E form indicates but, in the opinion of Hywel Wyn Owen, it may well be *myngul*, 'narrow or slender-necked'. The earliest form could stand for *tir fyngul*, 'narrow land'. The adjoining 'pass' would be *Bwlch y tir fyngul*, and eventually, with loss of *tir*, *Bwlch y Fyngul*. Late sps. certainly indicate the W def. art. *y*. An ancient road *Ffordd Fawr*, 'big road', passed through it over the Black Mountains.

**Bwlchyddinas** see **Dinas**

**Cadair Fawr** hill                                             SN 9712
*Cader fawr* 1832, *Cadairfawr* 1814

W *cadair*, *cader*, 'chair', and *mawr*, 'big, great'; because *cadair* is fem. its adj. *mawr* has mutated to produce *fawr* (pron. roughly 'vowr'). Heavily glaciated mountains were sometimes thought to resemble armchairs; compare Mynydd y Gader (see Black Mountains above).

**Caehopkin**                                                    SN 8212
*Cae Hopkin* c.1815, 1844; (tmt.) *Cae Hopkin*, (cottage) *Cae Hopkin bach*, 1803

From a farm: W *cae*, 'enclosure, field', and a W pers.n. derived from E *Hobbekin*, a diminutive of *Hob*, a pet form of Robert, and used in Wales since the 13thC (*Welsh Surnames*). The industrial settlement was called *Coalbrook* 1832 and marked as *Abercrafe Coal-works* 1814.

**Calfannog** ?SO 0125

*Mainaur Calvennauk,* ~ *Calvennauc* c.1150-75 (1351), *Kalvannauc* 1281, *CALVANNOK', Caluannok'* 1326 (1516)

Unidentified but it may be Heolfannog which is *Heol-fanog* 1832 and has been explained by one source in 1815 as *HEOLVANOG, or more correctly Aelvanog, the lofty brow. Calfannog* may mean 'horned or projecting tail or point' (*cal,* 'penis', and *bannog,* an adj. formed from *ban:* see Brecon Beacons), possibly referring to the ridge on which Heolfannog lies. If the identification is accurate, then *Heolfannog* may have arisen over a long period through misunderstanding: to say 'in Calfannog' a W speaker might have said 'ynghalfannog' (now written 'yng Nghalfannog'); this could have been construed as 'yn Halfannog' and finally misassociated with W *heol,* 'street, road', before *bannog.* This argument, however, has to remain theoretical until we possess more sps. of Heolfannog.

Calfannog was a grange of the bishop of St. David's.

**Callwen** SN 8416

*Capel Callwen* 1578,1798, *Capel Cellwen* 1832, *Cappel Callwen* 1744; (chp.) *ystradwallen* 1548, c.1554-60, *Stradwallen* 1553, *ystrad wallt twen* c.1566

A chapel-of-ease of Defynnog p. Generally explained as W *capel* and *Callwen,* 'Callwen's chp.', referring to a saint and virgin with her feast-day on 1 November. Her n. might be a compound of *call,* 'wise', and *gwen,* 'fair', etc. That, however, leaves the other sps. unexplained: these have W *ystrad,* 'valley, broad part of a valley', and a pers.n. *Gwallwen,* found in 'Bonedd yr Arwyr' (*Gwallwen ferch Afallach*). *Gwallwen* need not be a saint and the modern pn. may have arisen through misunderstanding: a chapel-of-ease at a place called *Ystradwallwen* (*Capel Ystradwallwen?*) may have been misinterpreted as 'chapel dedicated to Saint Callwen'.

**Cantref**  SO 0525

*Cantr'* 1372, *Cantref* 1402, 1798, *Cantreff* 1748, *p(lwyf) y Kantre* c.1566; *CANTREF al' LLANKENEDRE* 1404; (p. of) *S'ti Kenedr de Kantreff* 1514, *the Cantry* 1554

W *cantref*, literally 'hundred ts.', and roughly the same as an E administrative hundred. The p. Cantref derived its n. from Cantref Mawr (Cantref Tewdos) in which it lay. The church was dedicated to St. Cynidr, as at Llangynidr, which was replaced by Mary/Mair. Both saints are recorded in 1502 and 1565.

## Cantref Mawr see Cantref Tewdos

## Cantref Reservoir  SN 9915

Named from Cantref above; a reservoir constructed by Cardiff Corporation in 1892.

## Cantref Selyf (lost)

*Cantref Selif* 12thC, 1536-9; *Cantrefselyf* 1263, *Cantrecelly, -f* 1509, *Kantreselif* 1241, *kantre selyf* 15thC, *Cantrefselith* 1293, *Cantreselet* 1347, *kwmwd kantre sely* c.1566, *Tir Selyf* late 15thC

W *cantref* (as Cantref above) with the pers.n. *Selyf*, borrowed from Lat. *Salomo*, 'Solomon'. Brecon had a *Cantercelly ward* and *Cantercelly street* 1697, its n. persisting in that of an 18thC house in what is now called Lion Street. Cantref Selyf was probably once the greater part of the old kingdom or lp. of Brycheiniog north of the r. Usk but the n. was later confined to a commote in its eastern part. A very late 'tradition' asserts that Brycheiniog was divided before the coming of the Normans between Selyf, Tewdos and Einion, sons of Einion ap Gruffudd ab Elis; there is no reliable evidence of any Cantref Einion, though it was supposed to be the area around Talgarth.

**Cantref Tewdos, Cantref Mawr** (lost)

(hundred of) *Tewdas* 1299, *Cantref Theudo* 1536-9, *(Canteriva of) Teudas* 1299, *(o) gantref Teudos* late 14thC., Cantref *Mawr* 1584

*Cantref* as above with the W pers.n. *Tewdos*, borrowed from Latin *Theodosius*. It made up most of Brycheiniog, mainly south of the r. Usk, in contrast to Cantref Selyf on the north side. Like Cantref Selyf, the n. later came to mean a smaller area centred on Pencelli. The remainder of the original Cantref Tewdos came to be called *Cantref Mawr*, 'big hundred', possibly in contrast to Cantref Selyf cantref or commote.

**Capel Betws** see **Pen-pont**

**Capel Callwen** see **Callwen**

**Capel Coelbren** see **Coelbren**

**Capel Dyffryn Honddu or Upper Chapel: Capel Uchaf:**
SO 0040

*Capel defrune honthye* 1578, *Capel Dyffrin Honddu or Upper Chapel* 1798, *DYFFRYN-HONDDY UPPER* 1804

'Chp. in Dyffryn Honddu' with *capel* and *dyffryn*, 'valley', with the rn. *Honddu*, found also in *Aberhonddu*, the W n. of Brecon. Capel Dyffryn Honddu became *Upper* Chapel in contrast to the *Lower* Chapel at Llanfihangel Fechan; both were chapels-of-ease in Merthyr Cynog parish. Modern road-signs have adopted *Capel Uchaf* as a literal translation of *Upper Chapel*.

**Capel Glyn Collwyn** see **Glyncollwyn**

**Capel Illtud**
SO 9726

*Capel: ylldyt* 1578, *Capel Illtyd* 1832, *Capel Illtid* 1798, *Tir Llanylltyd* 1646, *Llanylltid* 1709, *Llanilltud in the Glyn* 1813, (hamlet) *GLYN, or CAPEL-YLLDYT* 1804

'Chp. of St. Illtud', a saint widely dedicated in south Wales, notably at Llanilltud Fawr (Llantwit Major) and Llanilltud Faerdre GLA. Formerly a chapel-of-ease to Llansbyddyd, an ecclesiastical district from 1884. There is a megalithic monument here called Bedd Illtud (SN 976262) called *Bedd Gwyl Illtud* 1842 (with *gŵyl*, 'feast, festival') and a hill Mynydd Illtud called *Mynydd Illtyd* 1832 (with *mynydd*, 'mountain').

### Capel Isaf see **Llanfihangel Fechan**

### Capel Maes-y-bwlch (lost)                                    SN 8434
*Maes-y-Bwlch* 1828, 1832

Earlier sps. not seen which is a little odd; if the sp. above is correct, then this chp. takes its n. from a former farm, now a part of the military range, called *Maes-y-bwlch*, 'the open-field near the pass or gap' with *maes* and *bwlch* (see Bwlch above). In 1764 there were no remains of a building but a local tradition and a sketch plan showing a gate *Clwyd y Cappel* and a *Cwm y Cappel* ('the chp. gate' and 'the chp. valley') indicate that it was near or on the farm holding. See 'The Affair of Cefn Arthen' in Brych 25, p.23. Probably a former chapel-of-ease of Llandeilo'r Fân.

### Capel Nant-ddu see **Nant-ddu**

### Capel Rhyd-briw                                             SN 9229
*Capell Rydd Bryw in Llywel, Ryd Bryw Chapel, Capel ridbrue* 1578, *Cappel Rhydbrue* 1798, *Capel Rhyd-y-brew* 1832, *Redbryuu* 1536-9, *Rheedy Brue* 1754, (mill) *Ridbrew* 1372, (messuage) *Tyr Penpont Ryd Brywe* 1569

*Capel* meaning 'chapel-of-ease (to Llywel)' and *rhyd*, 'ford', with either *briw*, 'broken, shattered', or more probably *bryw*, 'lively, vigorous'.The first explanation was favoured by John Leland, the antiquarian, c.1536-9 since he says *Redbryuu (Redbreu, i.e.*

*vadum fractum)'*. Some sps. have the W def. art. *y* representing the 'obscure' vowel which has intervened between the *d* (made by the tongue against the palate) and *b* (a sound made by the lips), probably to separate the two sounds. *Tyr Penpont* 1569 probably refers to land (*tir*) of the Pen-pont estate rather than to any bridge (*pont*) at Rhyd-briw. The first ref. to a bridge here seems to be *Rhyd y briw bridge* 1815. There is a castle here called Castell Du, given as *Rhyd y briw Castle* 1809 and it may be *Ridbriu, Ritu Pryw, Rotpriw* 1271. The chp. is now in the middle of Sennybridge military camp.

**Capel Senni** (lost)                         SN 9223
*Capel Senny* 1578, *Senny* 1754, (ht.) *SENNY* 1804, (lands belonging to the) *Chapel of St. Michael* 1537

Probably a former chapel-of-ease (of Defynnog) or a religious settlement, earlier with the n. and dedication to St. Michael. Situated just to the south of the present hamlet of Heol Senni, its demise appears to have occurred following the Dissolution. The rn. is found in *Dolysene* 1295 and as *Senny, -ey* 1540s; *Senny R.* 1754 and in *Sennye Mill* 1651 and *Aler* [=*Aber*] *Senny Castr* 1754 and *Abersenny* 1773. It could be a pers.n. as in *Tre-senni* (at Grosmont) MON. *Sen-* may also be found in the rn. *Sannan* CRM and *Llansannan* DNB, possibly meaning 'holy' (from the same 'root' as Latin *sanctus*).

**Capel Taf Fechan** (lost)                    SO 0513
*Capel taueechan* 1578, *Cappell Tavechan* 1720, *Capel-taf-fechan* 1832

'Chapel-of-ease near the little r. Taf'; for *Taf* see Taf Fawr below. The chp. is now under the waters of Taf Fechan Reservoir constructed by Merthyr Tydfil County Borough.

**Capel Uchaf** see **Capel Dyffryn Honddu**

**Capel y Ffin**                                         SO 2531

*Capel a fyne* 1578, *Capel ~, Kapel y ffin* c.1700, *Capel-y-ffin* 1778, *Cappel y feene* 1684, (t.) *CHAPPEL-Y-FAEN* 1804

'Chapel-of-ease near a boundary', with *capel*, def.art. *y*, and *ffin*, a word borrowed from Lat *finum* (like F *fin*). It is likely to refer to the boundary between Llandaf and St. David's dioceses and between the lps. of Hay and Ewias HER. The site of an early Baptist chp. and a Benedictine monastery founded by the Rev. Lyne (Father Ignatius) 1869-70.

**Capel y Rhos** *see* **Ciltalgarth**

**Carnau Gwys** hill                                     SN 8120

No sps. seen; probably W *carnau*, pl. of *carn*, 'cairn, barrow, mound', def.art. *y*, and *gwŷs*, 'pig; sow', probably referring to the r. Gwys Fawr which rises about a mile south-west of the hill. On the west side of Carnau Gwys is thr r. Twrch (*twrch*, 'boar') and Brest Twrch, 'boar's breast', a slope running down to the r.

**Carreg Lem** hill                                      SN 8017

No sps. seen; probably W *carreg*, 'stone, rock', and *llem* (mutated to *lem*), the fem. form of *llym*, 'sharp, acute', etc. This area is notably rocky.

**Carreg Lwyd** hill                                     SN 8615
*Cerreg-llwyd* 1832

W *carreg* and *llwyd*, 'grey, pale brown' as well as 'holy'. Like Carreg-lem it refers to a notably rocky hill and is likely to mean 'rocky hill, crag' rather than a specific boulder.

**Castell Coch**                                          SN 9314
*Castell-Coch 1832, Cas. Coch 1886*

Literally, 'red castle', with *castell*, 'castle', and *coch*, 'red, crimson'; a small castle, the line of its walls marked by fallen red stones. It may be 13thC or earlier.

**Castell Dinas** see **Dinas**

**Castell Einion Sais** (lost)                            SN 9728
*Castle Inon Sais 1698, Castle ynon sais 1693, (messuage) Tyr John Lewis, alias CASTELL EINION SAIS 1783; Cae Castell, otherwise Castell Eynon Sais 1864*

'Castle belonging to Einion Sais'. Hugh Thomas 1698 says that the castle was built by Einion Sais, a son of Rhys ap Hywel, lord of Aberllynfi. Einion Sais was a member of a family descended from one of the lines of princes of Brycheiniog. We know that he lived about the mid 13thC and that he and his descendants supported the Anglo-Norman lords of Brecknock, sometimes at great personal cost. One of his great-grandsons, Dafydd Gam, was killed at the battle of Agincourt 1415 fighting for Henry V who was also lord of Brecknock. See also Capel Rhyd-briw above.

**Castell Madog**                                         SO 0236
*Castell madock 1602, Castlemadock 1754, Castell-madog 1778; Castle Madoc 1796*

'Madog's castle'. Madog has been identified with the third brother of Bleddyn ap Maenarch or the third son of Dafydd ap Rhys y Ddimau but the sps. are too late to help. *Madog* was a very common pers.n. in medieval Wales. There were two castles here, one directly behind the present mansion, the former home of Charles Powel, antiquary, built in 1588. There was an identical pn. in Llandyfaelog implied by *Tir Castell Madock 1643*, and another in Senni now known as Nant-moch.

**Castell y Geifr** hill                                    SN 8216
*Castell y geifr* 1819, 1832

Literally 'the goats' castle', but there is no castle here so that the
n. must be fanciful: 'a hill suitable only for goats', perhaps. E
*castle* was sometimes used in this way and Breton *kastell* could
mean a 'steep rock' as well as 'castle, château'. A second use of
this n. is found on the Great Forest of Brecknock enclosure map
1819, probably applying to a cairn at SN 8621. Again the precise
significance is uncertain.

**Cathedin**                                               SO 1425
*Kethedin* 1143-54, 1596-7, *Ketheden* 1578, *Kethedyn* 1331, 1382,
*Kathedine* 1617, *(o) Gethedin* 1778, *mighaleschurch in Kethedyn*
1382, *Llanuihengle (Michael) Kethedine* 1536-9

Very uncertain; possibly 'cats' fort' with W *cathau* and *din*, 'city,
fort, fortress' etc., but it is difficult to find anything comparable.
The pn. bears a rough resemblance to pns. such as Dunoding,
Glywysing, 'land of Dunawd, land of Glywys', but we have not
found any early examples of Cathedin with *-ing*. If there is a
pers.n. here it seems to be *Cathed* or *Cethed*. Cathedin may have
had the alternative n. *Llan y Deuddeg Saint*, 'church of the twelve
saints', which occurs in the Book of Llandaf 12thC but the
evidence is inconclusive.

**Cefn-brith**                                             SN 9145
*Tyr Keven brith* 1680, *Cefnbrith* c.1817, *Melin-cefn-brith* 1833,
*Ceven Brith* 1828, *Keven y Brydd* 1754

'Speckled ridge', with W *cefn*, 'back' and 'ridge' with *brith*,
'marked with different colours, speckled, grey'. The hill is now
called *Llwyn-yr-hebog*, 'the hawk's grove', from a farm. The 1754
sp. may have resulted from confusion with an old inn called
*Tafarn-y-pridd* 1833, literally 'the earth tavern', near a ford over
the r. Irfon; this might well mean 'lowland tavern' in contrast to
the other drovers' inn *Tafarn-y-mynydd* (SN 918423), 'the

mountain tavern' on top of Mynydd Epynt. Cefn-brith is best known as the birthplace of John Penry (1563-93), the Puritan martyr.

**Cefn Coch** hill  SN 8253
*Cefn coch* 1833

'Red ridge, back', with W *cefn* and *coch*,'red, crimson'. There is an area marked *Rhyd-goch* (SN 827529) ('red ford') on the OS 1 in. map 1833 where a road from Abergwesyn to the Tywi valley passed over the stream *Nant-rhyd-goch*. The 'redness' may be that of the rocks. The whole area is now heavily forested.

**Cefncoedycymer**  SO 0308
*Coed y Cymer* 1813, *Coed y Cummar* 1798, *Cefn-coed-y-cymmer* 1832

W *cefn*, 'back, ridge', and *coed*, 'trees, wood', are often combined to mean 'wooded hill'; this is the 'wooded hill near the confluence (*cymer*)'; the last is recorded as *cymer* 12thC, and is the place where the rs. Taf and Taf Fechan meet. Most of the village occupies a promontory between them. It developed in the early 19thC as an industrial suburb of Merthyr Tudful and was transferred to it in 1974. The chapel-of-ease opened in 1874.

**Cefn Fannog** hill  SN 8251
*Cefn Ffanog* 1820-1, *Cefn fanog* 1833

'Prominent ridge or hill', with *cefn* (as above) and *bannog*, 'high; famous' as well as 'horned, turreted'.

**Cefn Gast** hill  SN 9147
(messuage) *Keven Gast* 1773, *Cefn gâst* 1820-1, *Cefn-gast* 1833

'Bitch's ridge', with *gast*, pl. *geist*, 'bitch' and 'harlot, whore'.

## Cefngorwydd                                     SN 9045

Named from *Gwarwydd* c.1817, 1838, *Tyr y gorwidd* 1680 at SN
905454. There is a ref. in the poetry of Cynddelw to *gorwyt epynt*
1155-1200 (early 14thC) which probably applies to this place. W
*gorwydd*, 'edge or border of woodland' and 'wooded slope';
with *cefn* as in Cefn-brith and Cefncoedycymer. The actual
ridge is called *Cefn Llanddewi* 1833 referring to Llanddewi
Llwynyfynwent below.

## Cefn Llwydlo hill                               SN 8542.
*CEFN LLWYDLO* 1832, *Cefn Llwydlo* 1828

W *cefn* as above and *Llwydlo* which is the W n. for Ludlow SHR.
Not far from the hill was Llwydlo Fach, spelt *Llwydlo vach* 1754,
*Ludlowvaugh House* 1698, meaning 'little Ludlow', which
Richard Fenton 1804-13 described as 'a small Ale House' where
suitors to the Court of Wales and the Marches used to meet. The
court frequently met at Ludlow but there seems to be no proof
that it ever met here. It is not uncommon for places in Wales to
have such transferred ns. and many appear to be old inns; some
may be mocking for remote places. Llwydlo Fach lay on an old
road, used by drovers, running from Tafarn y Pridd (see Cefn-
brith above) south-west through Cefn-gorwydd towards
Cynghordy CRM. Fenton's explanation may have been partly
inspired by *cynghordy*, 'counsel house, house where advice
could be obtained'.

## Cefn Mawr hill                                  SN 7915

No sps. seen though Greenwood's map 1828 appears to show a
house ?*Car Mawr*. W *cefn* as in Cefn Fannog, Cefn-gast, etc. and
*mawr*, 'big'. It forms a long ridge between the rs. Gwys Fawr
and Gïedd.

**Cefn Onneu** hill                           SO 1616
*Cefn Onneu* 1832, *Cefn-Blaen-Onney* 1786

W *cefn* and a rn. *Onneu*; see Aberonneu above.

**Cefnprysg** (lost)
*KEUYNPRESK'* 1326 (1516)

'Copse ridge': W *cefn* and *prys, -g*, 'brushwood, thicket, copse'.
A lost pn. in Garthbrengi or Trallwng.

**Cefnrhos** see **Gelli Talgarth**

**Cefn-y-bedd**                           SO 0051
*Keuenebeht* 1277, *Cavenabeth* 1720, (a little farmhouse) *Keven y
bedd* 1802, *KEVEN Y BEDH* 1600-7, *Cefn-y-bedd* 1833

W *cefn*,'ridge', def.art. *y* and *bedd*, 'grave'. Reputedly the place
where Llywelyn ap Gruffudd, prince of Wales, was killed in
1282, and commemorated by a monument placed here in 1956,
but the first ref. defeats any suggestion that this is the site of his
grave. *Cwm Llywelyn* ('Llywelyn's combe') appears on the OS
1in. map 1833 here, but the antiquity of the n. is unknown.
Other sources, in any case, say that his body was placed in the
monastery church at Cwm-hir RAD. Local tradition associates
Cefn-y-bedd with a prehistoric grave – that seems very likely.
The grid ref. above now applies to Cilmeri (see below), a n.
taken from Cilmeri farm, half a mile west of the hamlet.

**Cellywredd** (lost)
*Cellywredd* 1706

In Llanwrthwl. Sps. are so few that it is very difficult: can it be
W *celli*, 'grove, small wood', and *gwerdd*, 'green'? There are,
however, several references to a *Kylewrah* 1290, *Kilewrah* 1291
and *Kylewrath* 1299 in this area which – if they refer to this place
– would make our explanation impossible.

**Cenol** ?SO 1823

*Parcel Kenol 1786-7, Cenol Parcel 1851*

'Middle part (of the p. of Llanfihangel Cwm Du)' with *canol, cenol*, 'middle', and *parsel*, a fairly common n. for ts. and hamlets in CRD and MER, ie. subdivisions of ps.

**Cerrig Duon** SN 8520

*Cerrig-ddu (the Black Stones) 1886*

As above: the pl. *cerrig* of *carreg* (as in Carreg-lem, Carreg-lwyd above) and *duon*, which is the pl. of *du*, 'black, dark'. A prehistoric circle of stones.

**Chwefru** rn. SO 0052

*Hweuery 1278, Weuery R. 1695, Wheffrey 1754, River Whefri 1828, Cumwheuery 1290, 1291*

'Lively (r.)', with the el. found in *chwefrin, -s, -g*, 'wild' etc., and a suffix -*i* confused with -*u*. In south Wales the standard W *chw-* is generally pronounced *wh-* and plain *w-* as in *wharae, warae* (for *chwarae*), 'to play', and this is clearly shown in the sps. of Chwefru. It enters the r. Irfon near Builth at SO 032512

**Cilfaenor** SO 1724

*Kilvaynor 1222, c.1234-40, 1811, Cil-faenor 1832*

'Manor nook', with W *maenor*, 'a territorial division originally consisting of four (or more) *tref* units, (later) manor, estate' (B.G. Charles), as the qualifier. Despite its similarity, *maenor* is not borrowed from E *manor* or Lat *manerium*, although their meanings may have affected *maenor*.

**Cilian** SO 0742

*Cilyane 1809, Cil-ian 1833, Killyane domin' juxta Forestam Superior 1380*

Possibly W *cilan*, 'retreat, nook'. The n. of a former manor; the

62

house of this n. is called *Pwll-y-march* 1833, 'the horse's pit (or pool)'; *Cil-ian* 1833 is applied to a house half a mile to the east of the modern *Cillian*. Probably *Kyliev* 1271 (for *Kylien?*).

**Ciliau, Cilau**                                                    SO 2017
*Killey, the Kyliey* 1533-8, *the kyllye* 1597; *Killey Parcel* 1851, *Cile* c.1809, *Cil-le* 1832

W *cilau*, pl. of *cil*; the standard W pl. of *cil* is *ciliau*, but *cilau*, pronounced 'cil le' is more common in mid and west Wales, hence the sps. for c.1809 and 1832. There is no connection with *lle*, 'place'.

**Cilieni** rn.                                                      SN 9134
*Cilieni* early 12thC, *Killieny* 1556, *Kyllyeny* 1571, *Aberkiliene* 1622-3

Possibly *cil(i)an* as Cilian above and a suffix -*i* found in other rns. such as Chwefru above. Rises on Mynydd Epynt and enters the Usk at SN 9329.

**Cilmeri**                                                         SO 0051
*Kilmery* 1712, *Cilmery* 1886, *Cilmeri* 1820-1, 1833

W *cil*, 'retreat, corner, nook', often applied to remote or hidden places, and *mieri*, 'brambles' or a pers.n. *Meri* or *Mieri*. S.J. Williams has shown that unaccented -*i*- is often lost; compare Ciliau, Cilau above. *Cilmeri* is applied in 1833 to a farm half a mile west of the modern hamlet now called (and misspelt) *Cilmery*. The silliest explanation is that Cilmeri means '*Cil-Mary*, St. Mary's Church' (Rev. Thomas Morgan in *Origin of Place-Names*) as if it contains Ir *cill*!

**Cilonw**                                                          SO 2338
(half knight's fee) *Killonowe* 1522, (lp.) *Killonow* 1888-94, *Cilonw* 1832

Possibly W *cil* and a rn. *Onnw(y)* containing the same el. as W *onnen*, 'ash-tree'; *cil* sometimes has the particular sense of 'source of a r.' or 'area at the source of a r.'. The chapel-of-ease here is called *Capelbrengoran* on Saxton's map 1578 and many later maps such as Coltman's 1798 (*Capel Bengorum*) probably take their sps. from Saxton. It does not seem to occur in other sources. The pn., however, looks genuine: W *bryn*, 'hill', and *Gwran*, a well-attested pers.n., found also in Bryn-gwran ANG.

Either Cilonw or Glyn-fach (earlier Glyn-bwch) gave rise to the surname of Sir John Clanvow (?1341-91), poet and Lollard, best known as presumed author of 'The Cuckoo and the Nightingale', a celebrated late medieval E poem. See Glyn-fach below.

**Cilwhiballt** (Cilwhybert)                                   SO 0126
*Kilwhiban* 1373, 1521-2, *Kilwhibalt* 1372, *Kilwhyballt* 1454, *Kilwhibarth* 1832

Possibly *cil* (as above) and ?*chwiban* (pronounced *whiban* in many areas), 'a whistling, whistling noise', as in several places in PEM (B.G. Charles in PNPEM) but it is difficult to explain the modern sp. and those for 1372 and 1454 unless they have W *allt*, 'wooded slope'. The 1832 sp. is likely to be a product of association with W *garth* as in Alltmadryn above.

**Cilwych**                                                         SO 1420
*CÎL WYCH* 1811, *Cil-wych* 1832, *KILWICH* 1804, *Cilchwa*, *Cilchwafach* 1814

Presumably 'excellent nook', with W *cil* as above and *gwych*, 'excellent, fine, grand', but the sps. are very late. There is a Cil-wych in Llansbyddyd.

**Clawddmadog** (lost)                                     ?SN 8647
*CLAUDDMADOG* 1804, *CLAWDDMADOG* 1811, *Clawth Madog* 1823

The pn. is no longer current; Kelly's Directory 1895 says it was near St. David's church, Llanwrtyd. W *clawdd*, 'wall made of earth, dyke, earthwork' and 'ditch', and the pers.n. Madog found also in nearby *Llwyn Madoc* (*Llwyn-madoc* 1832) (SN 903528) which is 'Madog's grove' (with *llwyn*).

**Cledan** rn.                                                     SN 88745
*Aber Klydan* 1670-85, *Cledan* 1699, 1833, (houses) *Glan-cledan-fach*, ~ *-fawr* 1833

W *caled*, 'coarse, harsh; hard', and suffix *-an*, comparable with an identical rn., a tributary of Afon Garno MTG; this is *Nant Cleden*, ~ *Cledan* 1603-7. The hardness might refer to their rough nature or the presence of calcium carbonate in the water. The unstressed first syllable has lost its vowel *a* rather in the manner that spoken E sometimes loses the *a* in *calamity, c'lamity*. Enters the Irfon at SN 893460.

**Clydach**                                                        SO 2213
*Clydach Dee, Coyd Clydaugh* 1605-23, (r.) *Clidagh ddye* 1583, *The Clydach Iron Works* 1813, *Clydach* c.1814, 1832, *Cledaugh* c.1612, *Abercleddeu* 1754

A 19thC industrial village owing its existence to the late 18thC/early 19thC ironworks of the same n. Today the n. is applied to settlements on both sides of the r. Clydach, but until recent times, that on the north side was called *Cheltenham*, which replaced *Ffynnon-y-coed* (so spelt 1832), 'well at the wood, well with trees near it'. *Cheltenham* is likely to be a n. imported by immigrant workers; cf. *Bath Row*, a terrace of workers' cottages. *Clydach* is a rn. here, formerly *Clydach Ddu*, 'dark r. Clydach', perhaps because it flows over coal-measures. There are at least four other examples of the rn. in BRE. Clydach (→Usk SN 902292) near Sennybridge occurs as *Cloutac* 12thC, *Cledach R.* 1754 and Clydach (→Caerfanell SO 107215) near Tal-y-bont is *Cledagh* 1560 and in *Aberclydach* 1832. All rs. with this n. occur in south Wales – we know that Ir influence was

65

particularly strong in west Wales and some adjoining areas in the 5thC – and it may be a borrowing from Ir *clodach* or *cladach* meaning 'a stony shore', sometimes 'wild stream with rocky bed' (R.J. Thomas). Melville Richards suggested, when discussing Clydach GLA, that the W rns. probably indicate rs. flowing over stony beds.

### Coelbren                                            SN 8511
*Capel Coyelbryn* 1578, *Capel-coelbren* 1832, (p.) *Colbren* 1608-9, (fm.) *Tyre y Kolbren* 1503 (1553), (~) *Tir Colbren* 1797, (torrent) *Nant ye Keylbren* 1555

W *capel* in the sense of chapel-of-ease (to Ystradgynlais) and *coelbren*, a word composed of *coel*, 'belief, credence', and *pren*, 'stick', meaning 'lot, omen-stick', 'allotted share of patrimony' and 'inscribed piece of wood'. It is not easy to say which sense applies here but, as with several other chapels-of-ease in BRE, this could have taken the n. of the locality in which it was built.

### Corn Gafallt hill                                    SN 9464
*Corn Gafallt* 1820-1, *Corn Gafall* 1833

John Rhŷs quoted a passage from the *Mirabilia* in the 'History of the Britons' by Nennius 9thC describing a 'wonder' or *mirabile* in the district of Buellt (*Buelt*), viz. a heap of stones bearing the footprint of a dog called Cafall (*Cabal*), the hound of Arthur, left in chasing the wild pig Trwyd (*Troit*). The heap was called *Carn Cabal* or 'Cafall's cairn'. It was said that men came to take away stone for a day and a night and on the following day the stone bearing the footprint was still to be found on top of the heap. If we accept the connection with Corn Gafallt, then W *corn*, 'horn, point, cairn on a mountain top' (B.G. Charles) has replaced *carn*, 'cairn, barrow'.

### Craig-y-nos                                          SN 8415

The original house was built c.1842 by Rice Davies Powell, of the family from Glyn-llech, on a field Cae Bryn Melin Bach and, consequently, some early records refer to it as *Bryn Melyn*, 'yellow hill'. It is best known through its association with Adelina Patti (1843-1919), the opera singer, who bought the house in 1878. It means literally 'the night rock' or, in this case, 'dark rock', referring to a rocky outcrop which overshadows it named as 'that limestone rock called Graig y nos' near Pentre Cribarth, and recorded in the Great Forest of Brecknock enclosure award 1819.

### Cribarth SN 8214
*Mynith Crybarth* 1602, (farm) *Tir Dan Cribarth* c.1814, *Cribbarth* 1798, *Pentre- ~, Ty-cribarth*, (hill) *Cribarth* 1806, 1832

'Ridge with a crest': W *crib*, 'crest, summit' and 'comb' and *garth*, 'mountain-ridge, promontory'. *Crib* is often found in mountain ns., eg. *Crib Goch* on Snowdon. There is another *Cribarth* (SN 9552) near Llanafan Fawr spelled *Cribart* 1730, *Cribarth* 1833.

### Crucadarn SO 0842
*Crycathorne* 1538-44, *Crecadern* 1545, *Crucadern* 1567, *kruc kadarn before* c.1566, *Crickadarne* 1578, *Kricadarn* 1555, *Crigcadarn* 1568, *kraic kadarn* c.1566, *y Cerygcadarn* 1839, *Crukadan* 1443

W *crug* as in Crucywel below with *cadarn*, 'strong, powerful', (as in Cwmcadarn below); the *-g* in *crug* has 'hardened' (provected) through contact with *c-* in *cadarn*. The church is built on a sharp point of rock. Some sps. show misassociation with *craig*, 'rock, cliff', and *cerrig*, 'stones, rocks'.

### Crucywel, Crug-hywel: Crickhowell SO 2118
*Kirkcowell* 1291, *Crukhowel* 1343, *Crukhowell* 1281, *Cruc howel* 1291, *Crughowel* 1333, *Crecowel* 1578, *Creke-, Cregehouel* 1536-9, *Crikhoel* 1263, *Krichowel* c.1283, *Cryg Hywel* 1831, *Cerik:bowel* 1573-80, *Cerrig Howell* 1584

W *crug*, 'hillock, knoll' and 'cairn, heap', and the pers.n. *Hywel*, generally anglicised as *Howel(l)*. The -*g* has 'provected' before the *H*- and then this has been lost as the breath is drawn in to say the 'ow' of *Hywel*. *H*- is often dropped by W and E speakers in parts of nearby MON and GLA and this may have contributed to its disappearance. Road-signs give the W sp. as *Crug Hywel*.

The actual mound is generally thought to be the hill *Table Mountain* (*Table Hill* 1886, from its very small, flat top) north of the town (*Crug Hywel* 1832) but local people according to Archdeacon Payne 1806 used to call this *Mynydd y Begwn*, 'the beacon mountain', and *Cae Crugiau*, 'enclosure with mounds', referring to the small hill-fort on top of the hill. It is possible that the actual 'hillock, knoll' is the castle in the town; certainly, 'hillock' would be an appropriate n. for it. *Hywel* has not been identified with certainty though some antiquarians, quite without warrant, have suggested Hywel, 'king of Upper Gwent'.

**Crug Mawr** hill                                    SO 2622
*Crug-mawr* 1832, (cairn) *Pencrug mawr* 1816-17

'Big mound', referring to the hill, with *crug* as in Crucywel.

**Cwmcadarn**                                    SO 1935
*Cwm Kadarn* 1584, *Cwm-cadarn* 1832, *Cŏmecadan* 1380

W *cwm*, 'a deep, narrow valley, coomb' etc. and *cadarn*, 'strong, powerful', (as in Crucadarn) which seems a little odd but it may well be the original n. of what is now called *Velindre Brook*. *Cwm-cadarn* 1832 is now Lower Cwmcadarn; the present Upper Cwmcadarn is called *Cwm-daren* 1832, almost certainly in error.

**Cwm-du** see **Llanfihangel Cwm Du**

**Cwmgïedd**                                          SN 7811
*Cwm giadd* c.1814, *Cwmgiaidd* 1886, *Cwm Geath* 1828, *Graidd Brook* 1805, *River Gyedd* 1795

'Valley of the r. Gïedd'; we have not seen early sps. of these ns. but they may have W *giaidd*, 'cruel, savage, fierce', a suitable n. for a rough, turbulent r. The valley gives its n. to a 19thC village serving the growing industry of the district.

**Cwm Irfon**                                         SN 8549
*Cwm Yrfon* 1820-1, 1833, (hill) *Cefn cwm Yrfon* 1833

'Narrow valley of the r. Irfon'; see Irfon below. The hill has *cefn*, 'back, ridge'.

**Cwm-taf**

A natural feature in Faenor; see Taf below.

**Cwmtwrch Isaf, ~ Uchaf**                           SN 7610, 7511
*Cwmtwrch* 1841-81, *Cwm Twrch* 1886, (valley) *Cwm-twrch* 1892

W *cwm* and the rn. *Twrch* which means 'boar, wild boar', no doubt from its rushing nature as in the case of rs. called *Mochnant*, 'pig stream' or 'pig valley'. There is another r. *Twrch* MTG which has a tributary *Banwy* with W *banw*, 'young pig'. *Isaf* and *Uchaf* mean 'lower' and 'upper' and are 20thC additions distinguishing different parts of urbanisation in this valley.

**Cwrtllaca**                                         SO 0933
(capital messuage) *Court y Llacka* 1612-13, *COURT-Y-LLACKA FARM* 1796, (manor) *Cortylacka* 1689

This may be the manor called *Lake* 1380, 1549, 1566 though the first ref. gives it as an alias for *Hieston* (see Trehendre below). Possibly W *llaca*, 'dirt, mire', as in Pwll-llaca SN 963330 and

PEM, but there are E pns. around Cwrtllaca and its p. Llandyfalle so that we may have ME *lak(e), laca*, 'lake, stream', from OE *lacu* meaning 'small stream, watercourse'. W *cwrt*, 'court, mansion' and 'farmyard', etc., is borrowed from ME or OF *court. Cwrt* could also mean 'monastic grange'. The def.art. *y* may be intrusive.

### Cwrtygollen SO 2316
*Court y gollen* 1697, *Cwrt-y-gollen* 1832, *Court y kollen* 1730

W *cwrt* as above, def.art. *y*, and *collen*, 'hazel-tree'.

### Danyrogof SN 8316
*Tan yr ogof* 1832, *PORTH OGOF* 1815, (mess.) *Tyr Dan yr Ogof* 1774, *Tyr dan yr Ogove* 1729

The present pn. means 'under or below the cave', with *tan, dan*, 'under, below', def.art. *yr* and *ogof*, 'cave', and originates with the former farm just below the cave given as *Ogof yr Esgyrn*, 'the cave of the bones', on modern maps, and *Daren yr Ogof* 1809, *Tarren yr Ogof* 1814. The farm now forms a part of the Danyrogof Showcaves complex. There are a large number of caverns here in the carboniferous limestone.

### Darrenfelen SO 2212
*DAREN FELEN* 1851, *y Darenfelen* 1867

W *tarren*, 'knoll, rock, tump', referring to the rocky promontory above the r. Clydach occupied by this hamlet. Nearby Gellifelen (SO 2111) is (dingle) *Gelly ffelen* 1797, *Cwm Gelly felen* 1793, (colliery) *Gellivelen, -velin* 1794, *Gelli-felen* 1832. Both have W *melen*, mutated as *felen*, 'yellow', since both *tarren* and *celli*, 'grove, copse', are fem. ns.

**Defynnog**                                                    SN 9227
*Deuannoc* 1202-14, *Devennoc* 1254, c.1291, *Devennock* 1406,
*dyfynnoc* 15thC, *y ðyfynoc* c.1566, *y Ddyfynnog* 1778, *Devynnock*
1798, *Wennyoch* 1299, *de Vennok* 1372

This has not been satisfactorily explained: possibly 'territory (or
perhaps place) belonging to Dyfwn'; the pers.n. was favoured
by the scholars Egerton Phillimore and R.J. Thomas. *Dyfwn* and
the territorial suffix *-og* would produce *Dyfyn(n)og* and the first
'obscure' vowel *y* has been confused with *e*. The sps. with the
def.art. *y* suggest that the pn. was regarded as a fem. word. The
sps. with *-noc*, *-nock* show 'hardening' of *–g*, perhaps because
this syllable was not stressed. The pers.n. has been found in
12thC texts but there is no positive identification with this
locality. Sps. such as *Wennyoch* and, most clearly, *de Vennok*
display 'wrong division' in which initial *De-* is confused with
Latin *de*, 'of', and sometimes omitted. Some authorities and
organisations use the form *Defynog* for the village; others cling
to the anglicised *Devynnock*.

The church is dedicated to Cynog, a saint well-attested in BRE
(as Merthyr Cynog), and the 19thC county historians thought
that *Defynnog* derived from *Tref Cynog*, 'Cynog's dwelling', but
this, etymologically, is very doubtful and does not occur in
early sources.

**Dinam** see **Swydd Ddinan**

**Dinas**                                                       SO 1730
*Dynas* 1285-90, 1521, *Dinas Castel* 1536-9, *Cast: Dynas* 1578,
*Castell Dinas* 1798, (castle) *Bulkedinas* 1233 (c.1286)

W *dinas*, 'fortress' (as well as 'city, large town'), comparable
with Cornish *dynas*; both were often applied to prehistoric
hillforts. The castle here stands on the site of an Iron Age fort
near a pass (W *bwlch*), hence it was also called *Bwlchyddinas*:

*Bulkedinas* 1233 (c.1286), *Bulkedenas* 1275. See also Fforest (Talgarth) below.

**Drum Ddu** hill                                   SN 9660
Llanwrthwl/Llanafan Fawr
*Drum ddu* 1833, *Drim* 1820-1

'Black ridge or summit' with W *trum*, usually a masc.n., but the sp. with *D-* and the mutation of *du*, 'black, dark', to *Ddu* suggests it was sometimes fem.

**Drum Ddu** hill                                   SN 9744
Llangamarch
*Drum-ddu* 1833, *Pen-drim* c.1817

As Drum Ddu above; the c.1817 sp. has W *pen*, 'head', referring in all likelihood to its summit. This is the highest point of Mynydd Epynt. The nearby hill Trembyd is *Trembit Mountain* 1754, containing W ?*trem*, 'look, sight', as in *tremiant*, 'appearance, view': perhaps 'look-out point'?

**Drum yr Eira** hill                               SN 8559
*Drum yr Eira* 1820-1, *Drum yr eira* 1833

W *trum*, *drum*, as in Drum Ddu, with def.art. and *eira*, 'snow'. There are many other hills in north BRE with *drum*, eg. Drum Da-gwylltion (*Drum-da-gwyllton* 1833), Drum Nant-y-gorlan (*Drum-nant-y-gorlan* 1833) and Drum Nant-yr-helyg (*Drum-nant-yr-helig* 1833) with 'wild cattle' (*da* and *gwylltion*, 'wild' in pl. form), *nant*, 'stream', *cor(dd)lan*, 'fold, pen', and *helyg*, 'willow-trees'.

**Drygarn Fawr, ~ Fach** hills                      SN 8658, 8457
*Drygarn* 1833, 1860, *Drygarn bach* 1833; *DRUGARN HILL* 1828

Probably 'cairned, place of cairns' with W *try-*, an intensive prefix used to mean something exceptional or abundant, and *carn*, 'cairn'. Drygarn Fawr (*mawr*, 'big') has a crest of rocks and at least two prehistoric cairns surmounted by modern cairns built in the second half of the 19thC by the OS. Drygarn Fach is a smooth, rounded hill.

**r. Duhonw** see **Aberduhonw**

**r. Dulas**                                                                    SN 9491
*Delas* 1547, *Dylas flu:* 1578, *Tir blaen Deylus* 1619, *Dulas* 1612, *Tyr Aberdylas* 1721, *Aberdulas* 1765

'Black stream' with *du*, 'black, dark', and *glais*, 'brook, stream'. Enters r. Irfon at SN 955495. One of the most common rns. in Wales. In BRE alone we have Dulas (→Wye SO 230428), near Hay, which is *Dunelays* c.1270, *Dulas flu:* 1578, *ar lan di6leis* 15thC, Dulas (→Llynfi SO 127523), near Bronllys, which is *Dulais* 1833, Dulas (→Irfon SN 919470), near Tirabad.

**Dyffryn**                                                                    SO 0309
Faenor
*Blaen y Dyffryn, Godre yr Duffryn* 1828, *Blaen-dyffryn, Gadres Dyffryn* 1832, (hamlet) *DYFFRYN* 1804

W *dyffryn*, 'valley, vale' and often 'bottom or lowland part of a p.'. The first sp. has W *blaen*, 'uppermost part' etc., the second has *godre(f)*, 'bottom part of valley'.

**Dyffryn Crawnon**                                                            SO 1218
*the Duffrin* 1744, *Dyffryn-crawnon* 1832

W *dyffryn* as in Dyffryn above; with the r. Crawnon found in *Abercrawnon* 1558, *Cwm Crawnon* 1710-19. The r. is also likely to be *nant crafnant* 12thC and means 'wild-garlic stream' with W *cra(f)* and *nant*, 'valley, stream'. There is a r. Crafnant near Trefriw CRN. The change from -*f*- to -*w*- is quite common.

Dyffryn Crawnon lay partly in Llanddeti and partly in

Llangynidr ps. and both also had ts. called *Dyffryn* but the 'valley' here seems to refer to their lowland parts in the valley of the r. Usk. Note *LLANGYNIDER-DUFFRAIN* 1804.

## Dyffryn Honddu

*Dyffrynn Hothny* 1443, *Dyffryn Honddye* 1536-9, *diffryn honthy* 1600-7, *DYFFRYN-HONDDY* 1804

'Valley of r. Honddu'; for the rn., see Brecon.

## Dyfnant (lost) see Uwchdyfnant

## Eglwys Fesau (lost)

A reputed chapel-of-ease in Llangynidr parish. No sps. seen and it may well be a 'ghost-name' for Eglwys Iail.

## Eglwys Iail see Llangynidr

## Eglwys Oen Duw see Beulah

## Erwood: Erwd                                    SO 0942

*ERWOOD* (forest) 1616-20, *Erwd Farm* 1822, *Erwd* 1839, *Erwood* 1823, 1833, (bridge) *Pont Erwydd* c.1830

Now pron. locally to rhyme with E 'firwood' but the W sps. *Erwd* suggest that both W and E speakers pron. it as if it were E 'erood'. Without earlier sps. it is difficult to be certain: the n. may be E meaning 'eagle wood' (as *Erwood* at Ludlow and *Ernwood* SHR) unless that itself has been substituted for an original W (*Pont*) *Erwyd*. This would be identical to *Ponterwyd* CRD composed of W *pont*, 'bridge', and *erwydd*, 'rods, rails or poles': a 'bridge constructed of poles'?

**Esgair Garthen** hill                                    SN 8464
*Esgair garthen* 1820-1, *Esgair Garthen* 1833

W *esgair*, 'ridge', but without earlier sps. it is difficult to be certain about the second word. If the cited sps. are reliable then it appears to be W *carthen*, 'coarse cloth, blanket', but it is hard to understand what that would indicate, unless it refers to a dense layer of peat over the hill. S.J. Williams added *garthan*, 'encampment', according to Geiriadur Mawr, which is no better.

**Y Faenor: Vaynor**                                        SO 0410
*Veynor* 1373, *Vaynor* 1535, *Faenor* 1832, *Vaynorweyno* 1402, *Sci Winoci de VAYNOR* 1488, *maynor wino* c.1566, (p. of) *Sci. Gwynoci* 1481, (p.) *Gwinaw* 1337-8

W *maenor*, which seems to have had the original sense of 'chief's residence' and later 'group of villein *trefi* [townships]' as 'a division of a *cwmwd* [commote]', and later still confused with E *manor*. As a p., it may well have meant a group of ts. or some sort of territorial division. The n. is misspelt *Vaynor* on maps and road-signs. The second part of the pn. has been lost but is clearly *Wynno* (rather than *Gwynnog*), a mutated form of the n. of St. Gwynno, dedicated at nearby Llanwynno GLA. The church at Faenor is now ascribed to St. Gwenfrewi in error. Compare Faenor (Vaynor) MTG which is *Eueynor* 1338, *Vaynour* 1360 and Faenor RAD (*A Study of Radnorshire Place-Names*, p. 54).

**Y Fan Fawr** hill                                         SN 9619
*Brecknock Van* 1886

The hills in which Y Fan Fawr is the most prominent are called *Y-Fan-dringarth* 1832 and *VAN TRINGARTH* 1828 which suggest W *ban* as in Y Fan Gihirych and a rn. *Tringarth* which rises on Rhos Dringarth about a mile north-west of Y Fan Fawr. The rn. occurs as *Traugathe flu:* 1578, *Tringath Brook* 1828, and in

*Blaen-tringarth* 1832 but the sps. are too late for reliable interpretation. *Y Fan Fawr* has *mawr*, 'big'; *ban* is a fem. word which has mutated after its def.art. *Y* and caused mutation of *mawr* as its adj.

### Y Fan Gihirych hill                                    SN 8819
*Y-Fan-giharach* 1832, *VAN GYHERECH*, (r.) *Nant Gyherech* 1819

W *ban*, 'peak, point, beacon', and a rn. found also in *Pont-giharach* 1832 (SN 886212), which S.J. Williams interprets as *Cyhirych*, perhaps with Irish *cireach*, 'comb, crest', referring to the peak, or W *cyhyr*, 'muscle, sinew, flesh', and some suffix such as *-ach* (or *-ych*) found in other rns. It has to be said, however, that the sps. are very late and may not be reliable.

### Y Fan Llia hill                                        SN 9318
*VAN LLIA* 1819, 1828, *Y-Fan-llia* 1832

W *ban* as above and a rn. *Llia* which is (stream) *llya*, *tir aberllya* 1599, *Llia Brook* 1819, *Llia* 1832, *Llea* 1754, probably a pers.n. found in the Black Book of Carmarthen (late 13thC) as *Llia Gvitel* or a derivative of *llyfaf, llyaf: llyfu, llyo, llyu*, 'to lick, to lap' (GPC). There is a prehistoric stone Maen Llia near its source called *Maen Llia* 1815 and *Maen llia* 1828.

### Felindre                                               SO 1836
*Capel y felindra, Pentre y felindre* c.1700, *Velindre* 1744, 1828, *Felindre* 1832, *y Felindref* 1839

W *melin*, 'mill', and *tref* which meant originally 'homestead', later 'hamlet, village, t.' (and more recently 'town'). The pn. has mutated after a def.art *Y* which no longer appears in modern map sps. *Capel* refers to the chapel-of-ease (to Glasbury), *pentre(f)* is 'village'. The chp. was apparently used up to 1695 and then fell to ruin.

**Felin-fach**                                                                                            SO 0933
*Velin Vach Inn* 1798, *Vellinvach Inn* 1813, *Felin fach* c.1817, 1832

W *melin* as in Felindre and *bach*, 'little', mutating in the same
way as *tref* in Felindre because *melin* acts like an adj. causing *t*
to become *d* and *b* to become *f* (an E *v* sound). Felin-newydd
(following) is about two miles away.

**Felin-newydd**                                                                                          SO 1136
*Velyn Newith* 1513, *y Velyn newyth* 1546, (mill) *Velin Newydd*
1589, *Vellin Newydd* 1828, *New Mill* 1625

'New mill', now old! W *melin* as above and *newydd*, 'new'. A
mill on the r. Triffrwd.

**Y Fenni-fach**                                                                                          SO 0228
(Stephen of) *Benni* c.1143-54, *Benni* 11thC, *Benny* 1454, 1553-8,
*Benny wood* 1576, (wood) *Venni* 1813, *le Venne inferior* 1373, 1522,
*Vennivach* 1698, *Vennyvach* 1828, *Fenni-fach* 1832, (applied to hill)
*Coed-fenni* 1832, (Edith ~, Bernard de) *Benne* 1326 (15thC)

A difficult pn. which has been explained as *benni*, an alleged pl.
of *ban* (as in Y Fan Gihirych above) thought to occur in
Llangystennin Garth *Benni*, the W n. of Welsh Bicknor HER and
*Talbenny* PEM. W *bach* may have been added to distinguish this
place from *Y Fenni*, the W n. of Abergavenny MON, and must
be of some antiquity as the 1373 and 1522 sps. above have Latin
*inferior*, 'lesser, smaller'. The similarity of *Fenni, Benni* to
*Gobannium*, the Roman n. of Abergavenny, misled some
antiquarians such as Theophilus Jones to suppose that Y Gaer
through its proximity to Y Fenni-fach was the site of *Bannium*,
itself an erratic sp. of *Gobannium*.

The Roman fort of Y Gaer (W *caer*, 'fort') about 1½ miles to the
north-west (SO 0029) is thought to be the Roman *Cicutio*,
probably standing for British *\*Cicūtio* containing an el. thought
to be *cic-* found in Ir. *cich*, 'pap, breast', and W *cig*, 'meat, flesh'.
The n. very likely refers to the hill (on which there is an Iron

Age fort and the wood recorded as *Coed-fenni* 1832) between Y Gaer and Y Fenni-fach. Y Gaer as a pn. occurs as (waste city called) *Chaer, Carnois* c.1143-54, *y gaer* c.1600, *The Gare* 1698 and *Gare* 1703. Sps. such as *Carnois* and *Carneys* 1321-2 have not been explained satisfactorily and are too rare to be relied on. There are some fanciful tales given by John David Rhys c.1600, Hugh Thomas 1698 and Edward Lhuyd c.1700 associating Y Gaer with giants called Gogfran Gawr and Mwngmawr Drefi, the last appearing to mean 'Mwng of the great towns'.

**Ffawyddog, *(Ffwddog)*** SO 2018
*Pen-y-ffwddog* 1828, *Ffwddog* c.1916-17, *Ffawyddog, Pen-y-ffawyddog* 1832, (waste) *ffoothocke* 1633-9, *The Fothog* 1798

Probably 'place having beech-trees', with W *ffawydd* and a suffix *-og* found in adjs., often with plant ns. There is an identical pn. spelt *FFWDDOG 1832* which was once a detached part of HER west of Llanthony MON stretching along the BRE border, roughly six miles away from our Ffawyddog.

**Fforest: The Forest** SO 1828
(ht.) *FOREST* 1804, (ho.) *Cwm-fforest* 1832, *fforest Rynalld otherwise fforest Dynas, Greate fforest Dinas* 1561

W *fforest* meaning the same as E 'forest', generally 'hunting preserve' rather than specifically 'a wood', in this case belonging to Dinas above. Its alternative n. has the W pers.n. *Rheinallt* borrowed from AF *Reinald, Reynaud*.

**Fforest Fach** SN 9026
(forest) *Forest Vahan* 1326, *Fforest fach* 1832, *the little forest* 1540s, *the King's little Forest of Brecknock* 1570, *le litle forest of Brecknock* 1570, *paruam forestam* 1454, *parue foreste* 1372

W *bach*, 'small', mutated to *fach* after *fforest* which as a fem. word causes this change; 'small' in contrast to Fforest Fawr.

**Fforest Fawr: The Great Forest of Brecknock**     SN 81, 91
*foresta de Brechonie* c.1163-74, *the great Forest of Brekenok* 1536-9, *Great Forest of Brecknock* 1567, *the great fforrest* 1650, *Forest y Brenin* 1602, *magne foreste Brek'* 1372

W *fforest* as in Fforest and *mawr* (mutated like *bach* in Fforest Fach), 'big, great'; one of the largest hunting preserves in Wales belonging to the lords of Brecknock. The 1602 sp. has W *brenin*, 'king', as the forest was forfeited to Henry VIII by the Duke of Buckingham and remained as Crown property until its sale in 1819. The literary use of the W form *appears* to date from just after this sale but may be older.

**Fro**     SO 1519
Llangynidr
*LLANGYNIDER-URO* 1804, *Vro Parcel* 1851

W *bro*, mutated after a lost def.art. Y, meaning 'lowland' (also 'region, country') in contrast to the upland part of Llangynidr called Blaenau above. Note the W phrase *bro a bryn*, 'hill and vale'.

**Fro**     SO ?1220
Llanddeti
(ht.) *VRO 1804*

As Fro in Llangynidr.

**Gaer, Y** see **Y Fenni-fach** above.

**Gaer**     SO 1621
(place) *Gaer* 1624, *y Gaer* 1637, *Gaer* 1832, *The Gare* c.1700

'The fort': def. art. Y and *caer*, 'fortified place, fort' (later 'city'), referring to the small Roman fort at nearby Pen y Gaer (*Pen-y-gaer* 1832).

**Garn Caws** hill                                    SO 1216

No sps. seen. Probably W *carn*, 'cairn, barrow' etc. and *caws*, 'cheese', from its shape? or perhaps a shortening of *cawsai*, *cawsi*, 'causeway', an el. found in several BRE pns., and indicating a road or track. There are a number of trackways over the hills here.

**Garn Ddu** hill                                    SO 0212
*Carn-ddu* 1832

W *carn* and *du*, mutated to *ddu*, 'black, dark. Oddly found as *Carnblea* 1820-1.

**Garth**                                            SN 9549
near Llangamarch
*Garth Ho.* 1798, *Garth* 1804-13, 1820-1, *THE GARTH DEMESNE* 1823, *y Garth* 1778

W *garth*, 'mountain-ridge, promontory, hill', referring to the hill Garth Bank (*Garth* 1833) immediately to the north, or possibly *garth*, 'field, close, fold; fort' etc. The hamlet of Garth developed in the 19thC near the road bridge over the r. Dulas and Garth railway station.

**Garth**                                            SN 8113
Ystradgynlais
Garth 1538, (lp.) *Garth* 1795, (hamlet) *the Garth* (1801), farms *Garth Fm.*, ~ *uchaf* (hill) *Cefn y Garth* 1814

As Garth above. Today this n. describes a farm and its location but applied earlier to a hamlet in the p. of Ystradgynlais and probably a medieval lp.

**Garthbrengi**                                      SO 0433
*Garth bryngi brynn dewi* c.1180, *Garth bzyngi* c.1180 (early 14thC), *Carthpringii* 1283, *Carthprengy* 1281, *Kaerprengy* 1290, *Kardhprenghi* 1162 (1351), *Karprengy* c.1150-75 (1351), (rector of) *Carprengy* 1282, *Altbringy* 1671

Probably W *garth* as in Garth above and a pers.n. *Brengi* which also occurs in the lost *gallt brengy*, thought to be in Gwent, and the same as *Brenci* in the Bodmin Gospels c.1000. *Garth* has been confused in some sources with *caer*, 'fort' (see Y Gaer above), and *allt*, 'hillside, wooded slope'. The first ref. has W *bryn*, 'hill', and *Dewi*, 'David', the patron saint of Wales, dedicated in the church at Garthbrengi.

**Garthmadryn** (lost)
*Garthmatrun* 11thC, *Garthmathrinn* 13thC (16thC), *Garthmadryn* 1553-8, *Carthmadryn* 1372, *Carthemadron* 1454

W *garth* as in Garth above and probably a pers.n. *Madrun* rather than W *madryn*, 'fox'. There was a reputed saint Madrun but that is no proof of any dedication to her here. The pers.n. is thought to derive from that of a Celtic goddess *Matrōna*. Garthmadryn has been identified with Talgarth (below) because the Life of St. Cadog c.1100 says that Brychan's court (*curia*) *Garthmatrun* was at at a place called *Talgard*. This statement also lies behind the suggestion that Brycheiniog was anciently called Garthmadryn. One writer has even identified the *garth* with Mynydd Troed, a mountain three miles south of Talgarth. The difficulty is that the refs. for 1372 and 1454 indicate that Garthmadryn – or at least a place with the same n. – was in the lp. of Brecknock, probably near Brecon. Talgarth was not in this lp.

**Gelli**                                                                SO 0510
(ht. of *DYFFRYN, and*) *GELLI* 1804

W *cellj*, 'grove, copse, woodland', which is a fem. n. and has probably mutated after a lost def.art. (*c* to *g*). The n. also survives in (houses) *Penygelli*, ~ *fach* 1814, *Pen-y-gelli* 1832, 'head of the grove', with *pen* and def.art.

**Gellifelen** see **Darrenfelen**

**Gellifeinog** (Gellifaenog)                    SO 0937
(manor) *Gelly Veinocke* 1584, *Gellyveynog* 1722, (manor)
*Gelleyveynok* 1380, *Kellyvynock* 1544-5

'Stony grove', with *celli* as above and *meinog* adj., 'stony'.

**Gellitalgarth**                                SN 9455
*Kethitalgarth* 1578, 1610

W *celli* as above, *tal*, 'front, end' and *garth* as in Garth above,
'grove at end of a ridge'. A chapel-of-ease in Llanafan Fawr p.
which Poole 1886 says was between Bryn-ieuau and
Craigchwefru in Llanfihangel Bryn Pabuan on the hill *Lanferch*
(now *Lan Fach*), roughly at SJ 966572, but other evidence points
to a site near the hill Y Garth (*Garth* 1833) at about SN 943557.
Melville Richards gave *Rhos-y-capel* as an alternative n, meaning
'the chp. moor'; it is *CEFN RHÔS, or, RHÔS Y CAPEL* 1811.

**Gileston**
Llanfeugan                                       SO 1123
*Gilstonne* 1602, *Gilston* 1578, *Gileston or St. Cilly*, (house) *Lower
Gileston* 1747, *Gilson* 1760, *Chilston* 1698

B.G. Charles compared it with *Gileston* GLA which he says is
'Joel's farm' with OFr *Johel* and ME *-ton*. According to
Theophilus Jones, Bernard de Neufmarché, conqueror of
Brycheiniog, in the late 11thC granted Gileston to a certain Sir
Giles Pierrepoint but we have been unable to trace any other
ref. to this person. There is also an interesting mention of a
papal grant of an indult (or licence) in 1469 to William ap
Jankyn Gunter, 'lord of the place of St. Giles the Abbot (*de
Sancto Egidio abbate*)' which may refer to Gileston. The Gunter
family are usually associated with Tregunter and Trewalkin
below but there is a monument in the p. church of Llanfeugan
to a Lewis Gunter †1683. This may suggest that Gileston was
named after the saint for reasons which are now no longer
clear.

**Gilfach**                                              SN 9731
*GILUACH'* 1326 (1516)/(1526), *Gilfach-isaf,* ~ *-uchaf* 1832

W *cilfach,* 'corner, nook'; two fms. distinguished by *Isaf,* 'lower', and *Uchaf,* 'upper'.

**Gilwern**                                              SO 2414
(common) *Gilwern* 1810-16, (house and hill) *Gilwern* 1832, *Gilwen Hill* 1828

W *cil,* 'retreat, corner, nook' and *gwern,* 'alder-trees' and 'alder-grove, alder-marsh'; probably 'nook near alder-tree marsh'. The n. of an industrial town which developed after the appearance of the OS 1 in. map 1832 which records only the Beaufort Arms here. A station appears here on later printings of this map.

**Glangrwyne**                                          SO 2416
*Llangroyne* 1559, *Llangroyny* c.1814-20, *Llangrwyne* 1832, *LLANGRUNY* 1811, *llanygrwyne* late 16thC, *Langroney* 1610

Probably W *glan,* 'river-bank, brink' (if the modern sp. is correct) and the rn. *Grwyne* which occurs as *Groney flu:* 1578, *dýlatguerinou* early 12thC, and in the ns. of two hamlets *Grwyne Fawr,* ~ *Fach: Gronee Vaure,* ~ *Vaughan* 1607-8, *Gronovawr* c.1285-90, *GROYN-FAWR,* ~ *-FACH* 1804. S.J. Williams suggested that the rn. means '(river of) wet (places)' from OW *\*gweryneu,* later *grwynau,* with the el. *gweryn,* 'liquid, liquor', which may also be found in the rn. *Tryweryn* MER. *Glan* may have become confused with W *llan,* 'clearing' and 'churchyard, church', possibly because both words mutate after prepositions: 'to Glangrwyne' and 'to Llangrwyne' would both appear as *i Langrwyne.* Instances do occur, however, where *llan* appears with a rn. as in the case of *Llangefni* ANG and *Llanllyfni* CRN and it is noteworthy that sps. with *Glan–* do not seem to be evidenced before the 19thC.

**Glasbury** see *A Study of Radnorshire Place-Names,* p.57.

**Glasfynydd Forest**                                   SN 8524

(mountain called) *glas venydd* 1570, *Glas fynydd* 1832, *Glas Vynydd* 1813

'Green mountain', with W *glas*, 'green, verdant' and *mynydd*, 'mountain, moorland'.


**Glyn** see **Glyntarell**


**Glyn-bwch** see **Glyn-fach**


**Glyn Collwng**                                        SO 0717

*Chappell Glyncolloyn* late 16thC, (manor) *Glyn Colloyn* 1706, *Chapel Glyn collwyn* 1813, *Blaen Com Collwyn* 1602, *GLYN COLLWNG* 1832

W *glyn*, 'glen, dingle, (wooded) valley', and *collwyn*, 'hazel-grove'. Largely flooded by Tal-y-bont Reservoir. Capel Glyn Collwng (SO 078172), a chapel-of-ease of Llanfeugan, was demolished in 1973.


**Glyn-fach**                                           SO 2532

*glynn bwch* c.1510, *Glyn buch* c.1572, *Glynboughe* 1609-10, (lp.) *Glynbough in Wales* 1504, *Glynvache* 1652, (hamlet) *GLYN-FACH* 1804

W *glyn*, 'glen, dingle, (wooded) valley', and the rn. *Bwch*, spelt thus 1832, meaning 'buck, he-goat; roebuck', and probably found in *dýguarthafbuch* 12thC ('to the top of Bwch'). John Leland, the antiquary, 1536-9 calls it *Clindama* in which *-dama* is Latin *dama*, 'stag'. *Bwch* has become confused at quite a late date with *fach*, the mutated form of *bach*, 'small, little'.

Glyn-bwch or Cilonw (above) may have given rise to the surname *Clanvow* spelt *Clannon* 1313, *Clanevoue* 1316, *Clanevouz* 1322, *Clanwoe* 1324, *Clanvogh* 1321.

**Glyntarell (Glyn)**                                    SN 9722
*Glyntarth'* 1372, (t.) *Blayne Glyntatharell* 1584, *Glyn* 1692, *Glynne* 1697, (hamlet) *GLYN, or CAPEL-YLLDYT* 1804, *Glyntartaralth* 1454 (bridge of) *Tartharell* 1454, *Tyrtarelle Brooke, Tertarith* 1536-9, *Trwtarell* 1574, *Tatharell* 1584, *Pont Tretarrell* 1670-85, *Tarell* 1805, (land beyond) *Carterel* c.1150-75

'Valley of the r. Tarell': the rn. was earlier *Tardderell*, probably containing the same el. as *tarddu*, 'bubble, break out, run' and *tarddell*, 'spring, source'. The similarity in sound of -*ar*- and -*er*- has caused them to become fused and -*dd*- to disappear between them. See also Capel Illtud above.

**Glyntawe**                                            SN 8416
*Glentawen in Studgynles* 1559, *Glintawe* 1522, *Glintaway Mill* 1651, *Glyntawy* 1372, *Glyntawye* 1591-2, *Clintewye* c.1608-10

W *glyn* as in Glyn-fach above and the rn. *Tawe* (below). The former chapel-of-ease here is dedicated to *Callwen* (see Callwen above). Formed into a p. 1868 out of Glyntawe t. and parts of Llywel and Defynnog ps.

**Gorllwyn hill**                                       SN 9159
*Pen y Gorllwyn* 1820-1, *Pen-y-gorllwyn* 1833

If the present sp. is correct, then it is 'large wood'; *gor*- is used here as an intensive prefix meaning 'very, exceedingly', with *llwyn*, 'bush' etc. and 'grove, copse'; compare *gorallt*, 'precipitous cliff, hillside'; the remainder in the cited sps. have W *pen* and def.art. *y*. meaning 'top of'. *Gorllwyn* is also thought to occur in Llanfair *Orllwyn* CRD. Gorllwyn, however, is bare moorland, remote from any woodland, and our sps. are late: can it be an erratic form of *Gorllwm*, ie. *gor*- and *llwm*, 'very bare'?

**Grwyne Fawr, Grwyne Fechan** rns. see **Glangrwyne**

**Gurnos**                                          SN 7709

(common or pasture) *Gwernys* 1596, *Gurnose Mill* 1729, *Tir y Gyrnos* 1614, *Gyrnos* 1797, 1892, *Goytre Gwernos Farm, the Gwernos* 1787

There are similar ns. elsewhere, especially in south Wales, such as *Pen y Gurnos* (SN 7751) at Llanddewi Brefi CRD, *Gyrnos* (SN 9257) at Llanafan Fawr, and *Y Gyrn* (SN 9821) at Glyn, all applying to hills, and *Gurnos* (SN 6823) near Llandeilo Fawr CRM, and *Gurnos* (Merthyr Tudful) GLA. These ns. are generally thought to have W *curn, cyrn,* 'heap, mound; cone, rick', and a suffix *-os*, often found with plant-ns., such as *llwyfos*, 'place of elms', or *-os* used to mean something smaller, a diminutive, as *teios* (with *tai*, 'houses'), 'cottages', but this explanation may not apply here. The sps. for 1596 and 1787 suggest that we may have W *gwern*, 'alder-trees', which would make evident sense when we compare it with *llwyfos*; if the pn. has *curn, cyrn,* then we would have to explain *Gwernys, Gwernos* as mistaken associations with the plant-n. *gwern*. The topography also suits *gwern*. It is possible that *Gwer-* has developed into *Gwr-, Gyr-* rather in the manner that *Bedlwynog* has produced *Bedlinog* MON (*-lwyn-* to *-lin-*).

**Gwarafog**                                        SN 9548

*Goeravauk* 1290, 1291, *Goerawauc* 1291, *Goerafant* (*Goerafauc*) 1298-9, *GWARAFOG* 1804, 1851, *Gwaravog* 1779

Possibly W *gwar*, 'place just above, upper part, margin', a common el. in south Wales pns., though the two early sps. above bear a resemblance to W *gwêr*, 'shade'; the remainder *-awog, -afog* is uncertain.

**Gwaun Nant-ddu**                                  SO 0017

*Gwaun-nant-ddu* 1832, *Waun Nant-du* 1814

'Moor at black stream', with *gwaun*, 'moorland, heath', *nant*, earlier 'valley', later 'stream', and the adj. *du*, 'black, dark', applying to a natural feature.

**Gwaunygeifr** ?SO 1118
*Gwern-y-gafr* 1832

Uncertain, because of the late and equivocal sps.: 'moor of the goats' (if we accept the sp. in WATU with *gwaun* as above, def.art. *y* and *geifr*, pl. of *gafr*, 'goat, she-goat', but the 1832 sp. favours *gwern*, 'alder-trees' or 'place where alder-trees grow, ie. marsh'. It has been misidentified with Buckland above but it was probably around Bwlch-y-waun (*bwlch*, 'gap, pass'), Llanddeti. A former common *Waun y gyfir, Waun y geifr*, meaning the same, occurs in 1814 and 1832 (SO 082312) at Llanddew.

**Gwenddwr** SO 0643
(land of) *Wentorth* 1204-14, *Wendor* 1241, 1372, *Gwenthur* 1513, *Gwenthor* 1569, *gwen ðwr* c.1566

'White water', with *gwen*, 'white, fair' (and 'holy'), and *dwfr*, *dŵr*, 'water'. *Gwen* is the fem. form of *gwyn* and one would not normally expect it with *dŵr* which is masc. but there are exceptions to the rule as *gwenci* (*gwen* and *ci*, 'dog' etc.), 'weasel'; in addition, W *afon*, 'river', is fem. and as a rn. *Gwenddwr* may also have been regarded as fem.

**Gwerngoed Owen** (lost: in Llandyfalle)
*Gwen coed Owen* 1608, *Gwernegoed Owen* 1617

'Alder-trees or alder-tree wood associated with Owen', ie. *gwern* (see Gilwern above), *coed*, 'trees, wood', and the very common pers.n. *Owen, Owain* (from OW *Eugein*).

**Gwernvale** SO 2119

(capital messuage) *Gwern evaalde* 1518-29, (manor) *gwerne valde* 1594, *Gwernuald* c.1700, *Gwernyvale* 1608, *GWERNVALE* 1815

Note also Theophilus Jones's *Gwern y vale (anglicized) Gwernvale* 1809. The antiquarian Benjamin Heath Malkin 1807 says it takes its n. 'from a little streamlet, which passes through it'. This must be the r., unnamed on OS maps, which rises on the south side of Pen Cerrig Calch (SO 2121) and flows past Gwernvale to the r. Usk by Crucywel. There are references to property at *Twyn Kilvaley* 1753-1837 and *Pentwyn Valley* 1781-85 and to a common *Tonkin Valle* 1772-1829, all apparently applying to Twyn (SO 2112201) about 1/2 m. north of Gwernvale. On the basis of the available evidence the first el. must be W *gwern* (as in Gwerngoed Owen above) but it is too hazardous to attempt to explain *-vale, -valde, -valey*, etc. They are unlikely to contain *balau*, pl. of *bâl* (as in Mynydd Pen-y-fâl below), or anything similar because of the *-d(e)-* in three of the sps. above. *Gwernvale* is now pronounced with two syllables but the evidence suggests it earlier had at least three. The pn. has been wrongly explained as a corruption of *Tir Wronou Foel* (with *tir*, 'land, territory') because of a grant 1322 of certain property by a person of the n. *Wronon Voel*, comporcionary of St. Edmund's church, Crucywel. *Wronon Voel* appears to be the common W pers.n. *Gronw, Goronwy* and *moel, foel*, 'bald'.

**Gwernyfed** SO 1737, 1836

*Gwernevett* 1589, *Gwernyvett* 1595, *Gwernyvet Park* 1699, *GWERNE YEVED* 1600-7, *Gwern-y-fed* 1832

Probably the same as *Gwerneved* PEM which B.G. Charles explained as 'alder grove', ie. W *gwern* (as in Gwerngoed Owen above) or less likely *gwer-, gwor-*, an intensive prefix meaning much the same as E *over* in 'over-zealous' etc., and *nyfed* (OW *nimet*), 'grove'. S.J. Williams thought that it might derive ultimately from Brit *\*Vernonemeton* or *\*Vernemeton*, 'sanctuary among alder-trees' or 'great sanctuary'. He also suggested that the 'temple' or 'sanctuary' stood near the hillfort excavated in 1954 (SO 175376).

**Gwryd** hill                                      SN 9339
*Gwrhyd* 1832

W *gwryd*, 'fathom, the distance of two arms outstretched'. Ifor Williams noted the occurrence of *gwryd* with the ns. of heroes and saints in the sense of some fancied distance, often quite extraordinary, from finger-tip to finger-tip, though Melville Richards preferred 'a man's height'. The word is apparently used in some topographical sense. The hill is shaped like a figure eight and *gwryd* may have applied to the neck of land between the two raised parts of it. Cefn Gwrhyd (SN 7208) near Ystalyfera GLA has a roughly similar shape.

**Halfway**                                      SN 8332
*Halfway* 1832, 1840, *the Half-way House* 1845

'Half way' between Trecastell and Llandovery CRM referring to a tavern or staging-house on the road from Brecon to Llandovery. The n. appears to date from the early 19thC and was earlier *Tirymryson* thought to be be W *tir*, 'land, ground, territory', and *ymryson*, 'contention': 'disputed ground', perhaps because it lies near the border between BRE and CRM. There is a Halfway Inn (SN 1721) roughly halfway between Tretŵr and Bwlch.

**Hay: Y Gelli**                                      SO 2242
*Haya* c.1135-47, 1230, *Haia, Haiam* c.1200, (cas. of) *Haia taillata* 1121; *Tentura Haie* c.1150-75, *Haye* 1321-2, *La Haye* 1299, *Hay* 1578, *Hay.A. Celhy.B* 1573-80, *Hay (Gelly gandrill)* c.1625, *the hay* 1600-7, *a'r Gelli* 1215 (c.1400), *y gelli* c.1566, *y Gelli* 1778, *Sepes Inscissa* 1181-93

*Hay* (sometimes found as *The Hay*) is from OE *(ge)hæg* or more likely its derivative ME *hay*. Its original meaning was 'fence' but it came to mean 'part of a forest fenced off for hunting' and 'area within a fence, enclosure', perhaps referring originally to an enclosed area around the castle or, less likely, the later borough within walls mentioned by John Leland 1536-9. The F n. *La Haie Taillée* and Lat *Sepes Inscissa* are more problematic: both mean 'cut hedge, cut fence', although it is possible that the F n. is used in the same sense as *hay*. The W n. adds further difficulties: *celli*, with its def.art., *Y Gelli*, means 'grove, small wood', and some sps. have the addition *Gandryll*, ie. W *candryll* (*cant*, 'hundred', and *dryll*, 'piece') which has a number of meanings including 'shattered, shivered, ruinous', not quite the same thing as *taillée, taillata, inscissa*. It is very noticeable that W sps. with *Gandryll* are 17thC or later and it is possible that they are mistranslations. *Tentura* c.1150-75 seems to be unparalleled and R.W. Banks explained it as a form of Lat *tenetura* meaning the same as *tenementum*, 'tenement, holding', but it may well be a scribal error for *taillata*.

There is a mention of *hagan on hereforda* 958 but this cannot be proven to be Hay. There were two manors in the lp. of Hay: English Hay (*Haia Anglicana* 1522, *the Elysshe Hay* 1559) and Welsh Hay (*Haia Wallensis, Haye Wallensica* 1521-2, *Welsh Haye* 1561). The first was the area immediately around the borough, settled by E people using E custom.

### Hay Bluff hill                                    SO 2536

Apparently a modern n. shown at the W end of *Waun Llech* and *BLACK HILL* 1816-17. The first hill n. has W *gwaun*, 'high and wet level ground, moorland, heath' etc. and *llech*, 'slate'.

### Heol Senni                                       SN 9223
*Heol-senni* 1832

'Road by r. Senni': W *heol*, 'way, road, street'; for the rn. see

Capel Senni. This was the old road leading from Brecon to the Tawe valley.

**Hepste** rn.                                                           SN 9612
*Dyffryn Hepste* 1503, *Hepstey* 1754, *Hepsey flud* 1610, (hamlet of *NANT-DDÛ, and*) *HEPSTEA* 1804; *River Hepsteu* 1828, (r.) *Hepste, Blaen-hepste* 1832

Perhaps 'dry dark r.', with *hesb*, 'dried up', and *te(u)*, 'darkness'; the r. is periodically dry because it flows over porous carboniferous limestone. Enters the r. Mellte at SN 924099. Theophilus Jones says several rs. in this area were called *Hespin*.

**Honddu** rn. see **Brecon**

**Irfon** rn.
*Yrvon* 12thC, 1426, *Yruon flu:* 1578, *Irwon flu.* c.1570, *Irfon late* 15thC, (mills) *Aberirvon* 1360-7, (bridge) *Pont Orewyn* 1584

Uncertain, though it is similar to Irvine, Scotland, and may be pre-Celtic.

**Is-irfon** (lost)
*is Rivon* 1543, *is irvon* c.1566, *Isyrwon* 1584

W *is*, 'lower' and 'below, under', possibly in the sense 'nearer'; the n. of a commote or *swydd* in the cantref of Buellt (see Builth), probably identical to Swydd Irfon below.

**Libanus**                                                              SN 9925
*Libanus* 1828, 1840, 1851

A Latin form of the biblical *Lebanon* (in the prophecies of Isaiah 33.9) adopted for the W bible and used as the n. of many Nonconformist chps. throughout Wales. The village takes its n. from an Independent chp., built 1823, which was replaced by a United Reformed Church chp. in 1972 following road realignment. Shown as *Pont-clun* 1814, 1833; nearby Cwm-clun contains a rn. found in *Tir Blaenclyn* 1625, (r.) *Klin* 1650, *Blaen Cleen* 1769, *Penclun* 1814; this has the common south Wales el. *clun*, 'meadow, moor, brake, brushwood'.

### Llanafan Fawr                                           SN 9655

*Llanavan Vaur* c.1198-1214, *Lanavanvaur in Buelth* 1259, *Llananan Vaur* 1503, *ll.afan fawr* c.1566, (church of) *Sancti Avani quæ Britannice Lanavan* c.1200

'Church of Afan', with *llán*, 'a piece of consecrated ground, churchyard, church' (earlier 'clearing, open space') and the pers.n. *Afan*, presumably Afan Buellt in 12th-13thC manuscripts and a reputed bishop of Llanbadarn Fawr CRD. There was a *Ffynnon Afan*, 'Afan's well', here in 1699 and a *Derwen Afan*, 'Afan's oak-tree'. He is also dedicated at Llanafan Fechan below and Llanafan (Llanafan o'r Trawsgoed) CRD. *Mawr*, 'big', has been added to distinguish it from Llanafan Fechan.

### Llanafan Fechan (Llanfechan)                           SN 9750

*Llanauan vachan* 1578, *Lanavanveghan* 1682, *Llanvethan* 1563

As Llanafan above, with W *bechan*, mutated as *Fechan*, 'small', distinguishing it from 'big Llanafan'. The pn. is also found contracted as *Llanfechan*, with loss of *–afan-*. The contraction may well have been encouraged by casual omission of the first *–an-*, i.e. *Llanafan Fechan* > *Llanaf'fechan* > *Llanfechan*.

### Llanbedr Ystrad Yw                                      SO 2320

*in Istratyu . . . Lann petyr* 12thC, *Lanpetr'* c.1291, *ll.bedr ystrad yw* c.1566, *Peterchuch* 1578, *St. Peter by Crughoell* 1547

'Ch. of St. Peter in Ystrad Yw', with *llan* as in Llanafan Fawr, *Pedr* mutated as *-bedr* and the n. of the lp. Ystrad Yw (see below). *Peterchurch* etc. may be products of a cleric's scholarship rather than genuine pn.sps.

**Llanddegyman**                                        SO 1921
*Llandegemman* 1816-17, 1832

Poorly evidenced but likely to be W *llan* and a pers.n. *Degyman*
may be based on W *degwm*, 'tenth', according to Melville
Richards, or derived from Latin *Decumanus*. If the last is correct,
then it must be a late borrowing because an early one would
have eventually produced W *Degfan*. Decumanus is dedicated
at Rhoscrowther PEM where he is said to be buried.

**Llanddeti, Llanddetty**                               SO 1220
*Landetten* c.1291, *Landeitn* 1340, *LLANTHETT* 1496, *Llandettuy*
1513, *ll.ðetty* c.1566

W *llan*, 'church' etc. with a pers.n. but its correct sp. is
uncertain. Possibly 'church of Dedyw'; the early sps. with *-en*
and *-n* are almost certainly scribal errors because Med *u* and *n*
were very similar. *Llanddedyw* may have developed to
*Llanddetyw, Llanddety* through unvoicing or 'hardening' (*d* to *t*),
which is also found in nearby Llangatwg (from *Llangadog*), and
is a feature of other pns. in south-east Wales. The final *-w* is
often lost in W in a 'falling dipthong', ie. where two vowels are
pronounced together with the weight on the first vowel. There
was certainly a St. Dedyw, probably the same as St. Dettutus,
and *Detiu*, one of Cadog's three clerks (for Cadog, see
Llangatwg). In a manuscript dated c.1100 Saints *Dedyu* and
Clydog are named as the sons of Clydwyn son of Brychan.
Huw Cae Llwyd, a 15thC poet, mentions *Dedu fab*, 'Dedu the
son', in his poem 'Y Seintiau' ('the saints').

**Llanddew**                                            SO 0530
*Lando* c.1150-75, *Landu* 1201-2, *Landew* 1249, *Landou* 1281, 1326;
*Llann du6* 15thC, *LLANTHEW* 1804

'God's church', with *llan* and *Dwy(w)*, ModW *Duw*, as in
*Llandow* GLA and the old n. of Llandrindod RAD found as

*Landon* 1353, *Llandow* 1283, *Lando* c.1291 replaced by *Llandrindod* meaning 'church of the Holy Trinity' (see *A Study of Radnorshire Place-Names*, p.68). The modern sp. with *-ddew* may show the influence of *Dewi* (St. David) and the church is dedicated to St. David or the Holy Trinity; this was the site of a palace of the bishops of St. David's.

## Llanddewi Abergwesyn    SN 8552

*ll.ðewi    A.gwesyn    c.1566,    Llanddewi    Abergwessin    1572, Llanthewyeabergwessen* 1578

'Church of St. David at Abergwesyn (see above)', with *llan* and *Dewi*, mutated as *-ddewi*. *Dewi* is an early borrowing from Latin *Davidus*; the same n. was borrowed much later to produce *Dafydd*, another W n. for 'David'. St. David had a well *Ffynnon Ddewi* near the church. The p. was united with Llanfihangel Abergwesyn in 1865 and the church was subsequently abandoned and demolished in 1886; part still survived in 1909.

## Llanddewi Llwynyfynwent    SN 9043

*Llwyny Vinwent* 1754, *Llwyn y Vynwent* 1813, *Llwynyfynwent* c.1817

Earlier sps. not seen; as Llanddewi Abergwesyn with W *llwyn*, 'bush, plant' and collectively 'grove, copse', def.art. *y*, and *mynwent*, 'graveyard' as well as 'tomb, grave'. A former chapel-of-ease to Llangamarch.

## Llanddewi'r Cwm    SO 0348

(church of) *Sancti Davidis de Cum in Buelt* 1176-98, *Landewitum* 1252, *Landewycum* 1254, *Landewy Irtum* 1360-7, *Llandiwircombe* 1560, *ll.ðewi y kwm* c.1566

As Llanddewi Abergwesyn above, with def.art. *y*, 'affixed' to the vowel *i* as '*r*, and *cwm*, 'a deep, narrow valley, coomb, glen' etc., referring to Cwm Duhonwy. For *Buelt* see Builth above.

**Llanddulas** see **Tirabad**

**Llandefalle** see **Llandyfalle**

**Llandeilo'r Fân**                                                      SN 8934
*Llandeylo Gornagh* 1513, *ll.deilo ar faen* c.1566, *Llan Deilo ar Vawen*
1726, *Landerlo* 1506

'Church of St. Teilo on (Nant) Fawen', with *llan* and the pers.n.
*Teilo*, mutated as *-deilo*, *ar*, 'on', and the rn. This is *mauan* 12thC
and occurs in *Blaen-mawyn* 1832 and has been explained as a
pers.n. It may have W *maw-* thought to be related to Breton *mau*,
'agile, merry'. The sp. with *Gornagh* may have *corn*, 'horn', and
a suffix *-ach*, but what it applies to remains unclear. Llandeilo is
also thought to be *Lann Guruaet* 12thC containing a pers.n.
*Gurmaet* (?= ModW *Gwrfaeth*), found in the same source.

**Llandyfaelog Fach**                                                   SO 0332
*Llandeveylok in Diffrin hothenhey* 1398, *Llandevaylog vach* 1794,
*Llandevaillauc* 1215-22, *Llanvayloc* 13thC (16thC)

'Church of St. Tyfaelog'. *Fach*, 'little', distinguishes it from
Llandyfaelog Tre'r-graig. The pers.n. consists of W *ty*, 'thy',
used as a respectful form of address, and *maelog* containing
*mael*, 'prince'. Tyfaelog is recorded as a saint in Huw Cae
Llwyd's poem 'Y Seintiau' ('the Saints') late 15thC. See also
Dyffryn Honddu above. *Llanvayloc* (ModW *Llanfaelog*) may
have *Tyfaelog* without its prefix.

**Llandyfaelog Tre'r-graig**                                           SO 1229
*Llandevaylok Tref Crayg* 1535, *Llandevailoge-tre-ye-grack* 1595,
*LLANDEVAYLOG-TREF-GRAIG* 1804, *Laudyvayllock* 1310-11

As Llandyfaelog Fach above; it is very difficult to separate early
sps. for these two places, eg. *Landevaillauc* 1215-22, *Landeveilok*
1373. This is probably *Sepulchrum Rein filii Brachan* ('grave of
Rhain son of Brychan') *in Landeuailac* c.1200. The qualifying el.

has W *tref*, def.art. *y* 'affixed' as '*r* and *craig*, 'rock, cliff, crag': 't. at the cliff'. The church stands 'on a precipice' (Theophilus Jones). There is a ref. c.1475 to land called *tir Tyfaelawg*, said to be near Peutyn, in this p.

## Llandyfalle, Llandefalle                           SO 1035
*Landewathlan* 1263, *Landevathlan* 1241, *Landevathleir, -denalten* c.1291, *Llandefathew* 1778, *Llandevalle* 1553, 1557, *Lhan Dywalhe*, ~ *Dyvalle* c.1700, (land) *Laundenalth* 1380, *LLANVALLEN* 1400

'Church of St. Tyfalle'; *Tyfalle* may be the honorific prefix (as in Llandyfaelog Tr'e-graig above) and either *Ballai* or *Mallai* according to Richards (ETG p. 146). There have been attempts, all unconvincing, to identify him with *Tyfaelog, Maethlu* and even *Matthew*, the present phoney dedication. The pn. posed problems for E scribes who employed *-thl-* to stand for W *-ll-*; the sps. with *-an, -en* are likely to be errors for *-au, -eu*. The 1400 sp. appears to be a contracted form; compare Llandyfaelog Tre'r-graig above. The n. is spelt *Llandefalle* on OS maps and many official sources.

Llandyfalle Hill (SO 0737) is *Mynydd Llandefalle* 1832, with W *mynydd*, 'mountain'. Several local ps. have their own 'mountains', eg. *Mynydd Llanddew* (SO 0632), *Mynydd Garthbrengy* (a farm n. at SO 047348).

## Llaneglwys                                          SO 0638
*Nantegliis* 1524-5, *Nanteglus* 1241, *Lanegles, -eglous* 1372, *Llan Egloys* 1536-7, *Laneglois* 1554, *Laneglws* 1756, *Llaneglwys in Gwenthor* 1601

W *nant* and *eglwys* meaning 'stream near a church' or 'church near a stream' if *nant* is the qualifier rather than the generic. *Nant* has become confused with the common *llan*, a little odd since *eglwys* is a 'church' too. There are similar cases of confusion elsewhere, eg. *Nantcarfan > Llancarfan* GLA, *Nant Honddu > Llanthony* MON. The church stands beside Scithwern

Brook but the earlier n. may have been *Nant Eglwys* at least down to its junction with *Nant y Mynach* ('the monk's stream', from its association with land here held by Dore abbey HER); the farm of this n. is *Nant-y-mynach* 1832. The present settlement is *Llan-eglwys-uchaf* 1832 (SO 056387).

**Llaneigon (Llanigon)** SO 2139
(church of) *Sancti Eggiani* c.1150-75, ~ *Sancti Egyon* 1222, ~ *Sancto Eguino* 1254, *Llaneygan* c.1291, *Llan-*, *Llanneygon* 1340, *ll.eigion* c.1566, *Llanigon* 1620

'Church of St. Eigion', with *llan*. Eigion was reputedly born in Bronllys (*Brendlos*) and was son of Gwynllyw and brother of Cynidr and Cadog (see Llangynidr and Llangatwg below). He may also have been dedicated at Aberllynfi since Edward Lhuyd c.1700 names the saint there as *Gorgonius alias St. Eigan*. There was a Ffynnon *Eigion* (*ffynnon*, 'spout, well'), possibly the Boiling Well which lay between Crasswall HER and Hay, according to Francis Jones. OS maps have *-igon* but local pron. favours *-eigon*; in south Wales *-ion* is often spelt and pronounced as *-on*, eg. *Einion* as *Einon* in *Porteynon* (= *Portheinon*) GLA.

**Llanelieu** see **Llanelyw**

**Llanelli** SO 2314
*Llanelly* 1518-24, 1584, 1832, *ll.elli* c.1566, *Lanellie* 1595, *Llannelly* 1559

Identical to *Llanelli* CRM: 'church of St. Elli', a saint recorded in the Life of St. Cadog c.1100, and mentioned in Huw Cae Llwyd's poem 'Y Seintiau' ('the Saints') late 15thC. Unfamiliarity led to the church being misattributed to Ellyw and Almeda (cf. Llanfilo below). Refs. to Llanelli are late and it has been suggested that it was a chapel-of-ease of Llangatwg. Llanelli was transferred to Blaenau Gwent in 1974.

**Llanelyw, Llanelieu**                                    SO 1834

*Langeleu* 1143-54, 1310, *Langelen* 1321-2, *Langelew, -ow* c.1285-90,
*Langellou* 1331, *LLANELIW* 1482, *Llannelvewe* 1561, *Llanelewyth*
. . . *by Talgarth* 1406, *Llaneliw* c.1816-17, *Llanelyw* 1587

A difficult pn.: the meaning and even the correct sp. are
uncertain. Coltman's map 1798 and OS maps from 1832 have
spelt it *Llanelieu* while Elwyn Davies and Melville Richards
preferred *Llaneleu* in their lists but most sps. lend little support.
The later sps. (from 1406) suggest that we may have W *llan* in
its usual sense 'church enclosure, church' and, since the poet
Huw Cae Llwyd late 15thC mentions a saint *Eluw* and says that
the church here was dedicated to *Ellyw* (the present dedication),
then we might conclude that it means simply 'church.
dedicated to (St.) Elyw (or Eluw)'. The greatest difficulty,
however, is that earlier sps. contain a –*g*-. Taken at face value
that might suggest that the second el. is not *Elyw* but *Celyw*,
*celyw*, since *llan* usually causes a soft mut. in certain letters (*b* to
*f*, *c* to *g*, *d* to *dd*, *g* disappears, etc.); unfortunately, there seems to
be no evidence of any pers.n. *Celyw* and *celyw* does not appear
in dictionaries. Alternatively, the second el. might be *Gelyw*,
*gelyw* because our early sps. come from E sources which
sometimes omit muts. (see Llanfilo below for other examples);
again, there seems to be no proof of any pers.n. *Gelyw*. There is,
however, a stream here recorded as *Nant Elwe* 1561. In form,
that is reminiscent of the rn. *Elwy* DNB (found in *Llanelwy* or St
Asaph) but it could stand for *Gelyw*: *nant* is a fem. n., like *llan*,
and sometimes causes a qualifier to soft mutate (eg. Nant *Ddu*,
Nant *Fawr*, etc.): *llan* + *Gelyw* would become *Llanelyw* and *nant*
+ *Gelyw* would become *Nant Elyw*. Do we really have 'church
near (a stream called) Gelyw'? *Gelyw* could have a similar
meaning to the rn. *Gele* DNB thought to contain W *gelau*, *gele*,
'blade, weapon, spear', perhaps describing a r. which cuts into
the landscape. As for St Elyw, is he another 'saint' supposed
through misinterpreting a pn.? There was certainly some
confusion about the dedication of the church; one source cited

by Theophilus Jones ascribes it to a St *Kelline*; the pn. deserves further investigation.

## Llan-faes                                          SO 0328

(church of) *Launvays by Bregenogh* 1280, *Lameis* c.1163-74, *Landmais* c.1100, *Lanmais* c.1203-14, *Lannvays* 1239, *llann uaes* c.1180 (c.1400), (battle) *Gueith Lannmaes* 817 (c.1000), (priest of) *Lameis* mid 12thC (1351)

'Church in open country', with *llan*, as above, and *maes*, mutated as *-faes*. W *maes* now generally means 'field' but it earlier meant 'open country as opposed to woodland, expanse of open land' etc. (GPC), and the sense survives in W *tu maes*, 'outside'. The church is dedicated to Dewi/David, hence occasional sps. such as *ll.vaes dewi* c.1566 and *St. David juxta Brecon* 1535. Ieuan ap Huw Cae Llwyd late 15thC in his poem to Brecon ('I Aberhodni') has *Llys a gynneil pob eilfyw, / Llan-faes gorau lle in fyw*. Local people generally pron. the pn. 'Lanvês' rhyming with E 'trace'.

## Llanfair                                           SO 2019

(chp. of) *S. Mariae de Cruco-hel* c.1200, *Llanver* 1754, *Lanvers home* 1608, *Welsh Llanfair* 1813

'Church of St. Mary ', with *llan* and *Mair*, 'Mary'. It is said to have been the church used before St. Edmund's, the p. church of Crucywel (Crickhowell), thought to have been built c.1303. The ruins of St. Mary's were visible 'Till very lately' according to Archdeacon Payne 1806. The sp. with *home* 1608 is unexplained.

## Llanfeugan, Llanfigan                              SO 0824

(church of) *St. Meugan* 1251, ~ *Sco. Moygano* 1513, (rector of) *St. Meugan* 1313, *Llan Migan* 1522, *ll.feygan* c.1566, *Llanvigan* 1558

'Church of St. Meugan': *llan* and perhaps the same saint Meugan dedicated at Llanrhydd DNB, Capel Meugan ANG and Llanfeugan PEM, and mentioned by Huw Cae Llwyd late 15thC as *Meigan* in 'Y Seintiau' ('the Saints'). A *Mevgant ap Kyndaf* is recorded in 'Bonedd y Saint' 12thC (16thC). The present map sp. *Llanfigan* seems to be a very late development.

## Llanfihangel Abergwesyn                        SN 8552
*Llanyhangleabergwessen* 1578, *Llanvihangellabergoisen* 1672, *Llanvihangel Abergwessin* 1610

'Church of St. Michael at Abergwesyn': *llan* and *Mihangel*, 'Michael'; for *Abergwesyn* see Llanddewi Abergwesyn above. Some sps. represent *Llanihangel* in which *-f-* has been assimilated to the preceding *-n-*. W *Mihangel* derives from Latin *Michangelus* (*Michael* + *angelus*), 'Michael the angel'. A former chapel-of-ease united with Llanddewi Abergwesyn in 1865.

## Llanfihangel Brynpabuan                        SN 9856
*Llanvihangel Brynpabean* 1585, *Capel Llanihangle vrinpabon* 1578, *ll.V'el bryn payn* c.1566, *Llanvihangel pompren Bevan* 1773, *Llaniviblen* 1557, (lands in) *Bryn Pabean* 1578

'Church of St. Michael at Pabuan's hill': *llan* and *Mihangel* as above with *bryn*, 'hill', and a pers.n. which has not been satisfactorily explained. It may have the same el. seen in *Pabo* or *Papai*. The unfamiliarity of the pers.n. – to W as well as E speakers - created some bizarre sps. and explanations. The local 'explanation' was that it had *Pab Ieuan*, 'Pope John'. *Llaniviblen* seems to be a particularly bad writing error rather than a genuine contracted sp. The 1773 sp. has mixed up *Brynpabuan* with W *pompren*, 'footbridge', and the surname *Bevan*.

## Llanfihangel Cwm Du                        SO 1823
(Robert Clement of) *Miheleschurche* 1331, *Myghhelchirche* 1403, (church of) *Sancti Michaelis* c.1150, *S. Michael by Stretdewy* 1340, *St. Michael de Stradewy* c.1234, *SCI' MICHIS' de COME DUY* 1407, *St. Michael Cwm Du* 1798, *Llanfihangel Cwm-du* 1832,

*llanvihangell Cumddee* 1600-7, *Cwmde* 1383, *Lann mihacgel meibion gratlaun, Lann Michacgel trefceriav* 12thC

As Llanfihangel Abergwesyn with *cwm* and *du*, 'black, dark', presumably referring to the narrow valley of the r. Rhiangoll, though Theophilus Jones thought that it was not a good description. *Stretdewy* etc. is Ystrad Yw (below). The last two refs. seem to be unconfirmed in other sources and it is not certain that they both apply to this place. The first is 'sons of Gradlon' (W *meibion*, pl. of *mab*, 'son', with *Gratlaun* in MedW) and 'of the t. of Ceirio' (*tref*, 'township', later 'town', and a pers.n. composed of W *câr*, 'kinsman, friend', and terminal *-io*).

**Llanfihangel Fechan, Lower Chapel: Capel Isaf** SO 0235
*parochia Sancti Michaelis Parvi* 1503, *Llanyhangle uachan* 1578, *LL. vihangel vechan* c.1550-62, *Llanvihangel Vechan or Lower Chapel* 1798

'Little Llanfihangel' rather than 'little church of St. Michael', with *bechan* mutated as *fechan*, 'small, lesser', in contrast to Llanfihangel Nant Brân below. This is now generally called Lower Chapel/Capel Isaf in contrast to Upper Chapel/Capel Uchaf or Capel Dyffryn Honddu. Llanfihangel was a chapel-of-ease to Llandyfaelog Fach.

**Llanfihangel Nant Brân** SN 9434
*parochiam Sancti Michaelis de Nantbrane* 1503, *Llanvihangell Nantbrane* 1557, *LL. fihangel nant bran* c.1562, *LLANFIHANGEL-NANT-BRAEN* 1804, *Llanfihangel Nant-bran* 1832, *Nantbrane* 1538

As Llanfihangel Abergwesyn, etc. with the rn. *Nant Brân* which is *Bran, BRANE* 1326, *Nant-bran* 1832 and occurs in (manor) *Braan* 1379. W *brân* means 'crow, rook', probably referring to its darkness or lively nature, but it was also a pers.n.

**Llanfihangel Tal-y-llyn** SO 1128

*villa Sancti Michael* early 12thC, *Sci Michaelis juxta marā* 1486, *Lan Mihangel* c.1100, *Lannuhangel* 1321-2, *ll.V'el tal y llyn* c.1566, *Llanvyhangell-tallyn* 1672, *Llanfihangel tal y llyn* 1832, *Myghhelchirche* 1403

As Llanfihangel Abergwesyn, Llanfihangel Nant Brân etc. above, with W *tal*, 'front, end', def.art. *y* and *llyn*, 'lake, pool', referring to its·position near Llyn Syfaddan (Llan-gors Lake). *Lan Mihangel* c.1100 has been misidentified with Cathedin.

**Llanfilo** SO 1133

(Benedict of) *Lanbilio* c.1203-14, *Llanbilio* 1402, (William de) *Lambilso* 1234, *Lambilie* 1373, *Lanbiliauc* 1210-12, *Lanbylien* c.1291, *Ll. vilo* 1590-1, *Lamvilio* 1399, *ll.fillo* c.1566, (place) *Millewe* 1503

W *llan* and saint *Beilo* thought to be *Belyau*, 'daughter' of Brychan. The p. has *Ffynnon Filo*, 'well of Bilo' (W *ffynnon*, 'spout, well') and an *Allt Filo*, 'wooded slope of Bilo' (W *allt* as in Yr Allt above). The sp. *Millewe* 1502 must be a misinterpretation of *-filo* because both *m* and *b* usually mutate to *f* (a *v* sound) after a fem. n. There are examples of *llan* pns. which lose the *Llan-* and are called simply by their saint's n; see Llanfrynach following. The church has been wrongly said to be dedicated to Milburga, eldest daughter of Merewalh, king of Mercia (midland England), because of some slight resemblance to sps. such as *Millewe*. There are instances of W saints, unfamiliar to E scribes and clergy, being misassociated with E and universal saints, eg. Llanelli (Elli with Almeda).

**Llanfrynach** SO 0725

*Lanbernach* c.1291, *Lambernach* 1310, 1361, *Llanvernogh* 1503, *llanvernach, -virnach* 1600-7, *Llanvrynagh* 1513, *ll.frynach* c.1566, (ch. of) *SCI BERNACI juxta Brechon* 1408-9, *Bernok* 1373

W *llan*, 'church' etc., and saint *Brynach*, dedicated at Llanfrynach GLA and Llanfyrnach PEM which have similar sps. to our Llanfrynach. *Brynach* is among a number of BRE and RAD saints mentioned in Huw Cae Llwyd's poem 'Y Seintiau' late 15thC. His 'Life', thought to be 12thC, survives in a British Library Cotton manuscript and was published by Wade-Evans in 1944 (*Vitae Sanctorum Britanniae et Genealogiae*).

## Llangamarch (Llangamarch Wells)                                    SN 9347
*Langamarch 1249, 1339, Langammar 1328, Llangamarch 1339, llann gamarch 12thC (c.1400), Llangamarch in Beulthe 1547, Llangamarch ym myellt c.1592, Llangammarch 1833*

'Church by the r. Camarch'; the r. is found as *Camarch flu:* 1578, in *aber kammarch* (*aber*, 'confluence, mouth of a r.') 13thC (c.1400) and *Pont Gamarch* (*pont*, 'bridge', is fem. and causes the *C-* to become *G-*). It has *cam*, 'crooked, bent, winding', and *march*, 'horse, stallion', probably through some fancied movement of the r. There are numerous examples of rs. with similar ns. *Cam* as an adj. and *march* would become *Camfarch* with mutation and finally *Camarch* by 'assimilation' (loss of -*f*-). *Wells* was tacked on to the pn. because of its mineral (barium chloride) wells at the Lake Hotel, allegedly discovered in the early 19thC.

There is no saint Cadmarch or Cadfarch here, despite the church dedication; Edward Lhuyd c.1700 caused further confusion by suggesting St. *Cadferth*. The original saint was probably Tysilio since the poet Cynddelw (c.1155-1200) attributed the church to him in 'Cân Tysilio' ('song to Tysilio'). *Beulthe* and *myellt* refer to the cantref of Buellt in which Llangamarch lay (see Builth above).

## Llanganten                                                          SO 0051
*Langantein 1280, Langanten c.1291, 1418, Langanteu 1333, Llanganten 1833, llann gaenten 15thC*

W *llan* and a ?saint's n. *Canten*, allegedly a grandson of Brychan Brycheiniog (see Brecon), though we cannot find him in pedigrees. *Canten* may contain *cant*, 'edge, boundary', as in the pers.n. *Morgan(t)*, according to Melville Richards (ETG p. 175). The church is now dedicated to St. Catherine, a substitution like Milburga at Llanfilo and Almeda at Llanelli. It may have been dedicated to Cynog originally.

## Llangasty Tal-y-llyn SO 1326

(lands of) *Londeworne, altera Costinio* 1321-2, (church of) *SCI CASTANI juxta marā* 1486, *Llangasten* 1513, *Llangastey Talyllym* 1643, *Llangasty tal-y-llyn* 1832

'Church of Saint Casten (or Casteu): *llan* with an unidentified saint, possibly *Casau* (?*Castau*) in the poem 'Y Seintiau' of Huw Cae Llwyd late 15thC. If it has a pers.n. then its correct form is very uncertain. It need not be *Castan, -tain*, or some similar sp. with a final *-n*, because the first two sps. above have latinised forms, often written to fit standard Latin declensions. Theophilus Jones identified the saint with Gastayn, recorded in the pedigree tract 'Cognacio Brychan' 13thC as guardian of Cynog son of Brychan, but sps. make that very unlikely; one would certainly expect sps. - especially in later sources - such as *Llanastayn. Londeworne* is Llan-y-wern (below).

## Llangatwg, Llangattock SO 2117

*Lancadok* c.1291, (chp. of the Blessed Mary of) *Lancadoc* 1303 (c.1700), *LLANGADDOC* 1804, *Llangattok by Graghoell* 1412, *Llangattok juxta Curghowol* 1436, *Llangattoge Crickhowell* 1585, *ll.gattwc* c.1566, *Llancattooke* 1518-29, *Saynt Cadock alias llangattock next Crickhowell* 1552, *Ploeth Caduk* 1503

This may also be *llanngada6c* (followed by *llann uaes*, ie. Llanfaes, in the poetry of Gwynfardd Brycheiniog c.1180). 'Church of Saint Cadog (Catwg)', with *llan* as above and Cadog, brother of Cynidr (in Llangynidr) and Eigion (in Llaneigon). His well, *Ffynnon Gatwg*, is north-west of the church. Other dedications to him show a concentration in south-east Wales (note Llansbyddyd). The -d- in his n. has become -t- by 'hardening' or 'provection', a common feature in this area. *Ploeth Caduk* is a particularly interesting form, apparently having W *plwyf*, 'parish'; -th represents ModW -dd (pronounced like E -th in 'with') which is sometimes confused with -f (pronounced like E v) as in *Caerdydd* (Cardiff) GLA from *Caerdyf*, 'fort on the r. Taf'.

### Llangeneu, Llangenny　　　　　　　　　　　SO 2418
*ll.gene* c.1566, *Llangenye* 1578, *Llangeney* 1554, 1609-10, 1832, *Llangenny* 1547-51

'Church of Saint Ceneu', a local saint who occurs as *Cenau* in 'Y Seintiau' late 15thC. (see Llanelli and Llanfrynach), named by the editor as son of Coel Godebog, occurring in many medieval W pedigrees, and identified by Baring-Gould and Fisher as *Cenau, Confessor*; like Cadog he had a well (*Ffynnon Genau* in the sp. of Theophilus Jones). The meaning of his n. is uncertain though it may be W *cenau*, 'cub', thought to occur in other pers.ns. such as Gwrgenau and Morgenau. The sps. are curiously late, probably due to it having been a chapel-of-ease - often overlooked in many sources - to Llangatwg. Llangeneu has been identified with *Lann Cetguinn* ('ch. of ?Cedwyn') 12thC in the Book of Llandaf since it is named among four churches consecrated by Bishop Herewald of Llandaf (d. 1104) in Ystrad Yw, but the identification is unproven.

### Llan-goed　　　　　　　　　　　　　　　SO 1140
*Lann Coit* c.1150, *Lan goite* 1509, *o Langoed* 15thC, *Langoyt* 1380, 1444, *Langoyd*, --t 1373, *Llangoyde* 1567, *Llangot* 1464, 1494

Apparently, 'church by a wood': W *llan* and *coed*, 'trees, wood', but we have found no certain proof that there was a church here and it is possible that we have *llan* in its sense of 'clearing, open space': perhaps 'clearing surrounded by woodland'. There are very unreliable suggestions that Llangoed Castle (not a real castle) was built on the site of the 'white court' of Llys-wen (below). Llan-goed is in Llys-wen parish but Upper Llangoed at SO 113394 (*Llangoed* 1832) and Llanfawr SO 109403 (*Uppr. Llangoed* 1832) are in Llandyfalle p. The so-called 'font' near the hall is probably a prehistoric stone.

### Llan-gors                                         SO 1327
*Lann Cors* 12thC, *Lancors* 1198 (14thC), *Llancors* 1197 (14thC), (church of) *Sancti Paulini de Lancors* 1147-76, *ll.gors peylyn sant* c.1566, *Mara . . . otherwise Llangorse* 1739, *(Willelmus de) Mara* c.1127, *Mara* c.1210-12, (lands in) *La Mare* 1331

W *llan*, 'church', and *cors*, 'reeds' (a pl. of *corsen*, 'a reed'), and a sing. n. meaning 'marsh, bog', i.e. 'church in a place characterised by reeds', referring to its position near Llyn Syfaddan (Llan-gors Lake) below. The lake gives Llan-gors its alternative n. *Mara*, a Lat form of E *mere*. The church dedication is to Peulin, derived from Lat *Paulinus*, also dedicated at Caeo CRM. It is good to see that the anglicised sp. *Llangorse*, which falsely suggests an association with E 'gorse', is now dropped in favour of the one above.

### Llangynidr                                       SO 1519
*LLANKGENEDIRE*, *Llangenedre* 1398, *Llangeneder* 1535, *llangenider egloys Yayle* 1600-7, *Llangenyder Eglosyell* 1561, *LLANGENIDER & EGLUS YAILL* 1535, *Llangynyd* 1831, *Sco Kenedro* 1513

'Church of Saint Cynidr'; Cynidr was reputed in pedigrees to have been brother of Eigion (see Llaneigon) and Cadog (see Llangatwg) in a manuscript c.1200. There is a ref. to *Sco. Kened* c.1291 but this may refer to some other church dedicated to Cynidr in BRE such as Aberysgir or Glasbury. We know that he had other dedications in BRE at Llan-y-wern (now Mary) and Cantref, and Kenderchurch and perhaps Winforton HER. Llangynidr is often found in conjunction with Eglwys Iail which is: *Egglesseil* 1263, *Eglusseyll* c.1291, *Egloisieyle* 1517, *Eglesshey* 1559, probably meaning 'church by r. Iail' since the small stream near the church is called *Nant Yail* 1832. *Aber-yail* 1832 is shown at SO 169199. *Iail* might be a form of W *gwiail*, 'rods, reeds' etc., i.e. 'r. characterised by reeds, a river choked with reeds'. There is a similar pn. in ANG *Eglwys Ail* (alias Llangadwaladr) but in this case it might refer to the building materials (wattle) of a fence around the church or the church fabric itself (Tomos Roberts and Gwilym T. Jones in PNANG).

The reason for pairing *Llangynidr* with *Eglwys Iail* is not very clear unless the last served to distinguish it from other places called *Llangynidr* (see Cantref). More likely *Eglwys Iail* is an earlier n. for the church and p. or a church within the same enclosure.

**Llangynog**                                               SO 0246
*Capel Cunok* 1578, *Capel Llangunog* 1754, *Llangunnog* 1823, *Llangynog* 1833

'Church of Saint Cynog', with *llan* as above and a saint identified with Cynog ap Brychan (see Merthyr Cynog). The church is now a ruin but was formerly a chapel-of-ease to Llanganten. Identical to Llangynog MTG which is *Lankenauc* 1254, *Langenank* c.1291, *ll.gynog* c.1566.

**Llanhamlach**                                             SO 0926
(William of) *Lanhameloch* c.1203-14, *Lanhamelak* 1230-40, *Lanhamelach* 1188, c.1191, *Lanhankelok* 1373, *Llanhamlagh* 1378, 1448, (church of St. Peter of) *LLANHAMLAGH* 1486, *ll.hamwlch* c.1566, *LLANHAMULCH* 1600-7

W *llan* and a pers.n. thought to be *Anlach* or *Anlauch* (son of Coronac), father of Brychan Brycheiniog in medieval pedigrees, and reputedly buried before the porch of the church of Llansbyddyd (*Lanespetit*) 11thC, though the church is now dedicated to SS. Peter and Illtud. There is a Peterstone Court (so spelt 1832), a Ffynnon Illtud (*ffynnon*, 'spout, well') and cairn *Maen Illtid* 1832. The cairn may be the site of the so-called 'hermitage' of St. Illtud mentioned by Gerald of Wales c.1191. The pers.n. *Anlach* is not well-authenticated and deserves further investigation; Ifor Williams and Melville Richards preferred to derive the pn. from W *am* and *llwch*, '(church) near a pool (or marsh)', as in the case of *Amlwch* ANG (around a small cove). In both cases the middle -*h*- in *Llanhamlach* may be explained as a product of sharp exhalation before the stressed vowel -*a*-; similar examples are found elsewhere, eg. the W n. of Chirbury SHR *Llanffynhonwen* is composed of *llan, ffynnon* and *gwen* ('church at white well') with an -*h*- intruded before the -*o*-. The -*m*- in *Llanhamlach* is probably another example of confusion of -*n*- and -*m*-, found in both W and E.

Pron. now roughly corresponds to the map sp. but some sources, such as that for c.1566 show that it was also *Llanhamwlch* through a process called metathesis, ie. -*lach* becoming -*wlch*, in which the vowel shifts position. There may also have been genuine popular confusion or association with W *amlwch*, '(area) around a pool'.

**Llanigon** see **Llaneigon**

**Llanilid**                                   SN 8924
*Llanilid Chapel* 1813, *Capel Llanilid* 1832

'Church of Saint Ilid', probably Ilid or Ilud, a daughter of Brychan Brycheiniog. There is another Llanilid in GLA. The present structure dates from 1883 and coincides with Crai, a chapel-of-ease of Defynnog, becoming a separate ecclesiastical district. Prior to this there was a chp., said to have been of Celtic origin, close to today's Tirycapel (SN 8827), which was demolished c.1885.

**Llanilltud** see **Capel Illtud**

## Llanllywenfel, Llanlleonfel                         SN 9349

*Lanloeluayl* 1280, *Llanllewenvoyl* 1360-7, *Llanlloenvell'* 1513, *ll.llywen fel* c.1566, *Llanllywenvell* 1586, *Llanlloenwell* 1671, *LLANLLEONWELL* 1804, *Llanlloweluyn* 1421, *Llanlleonfel* 1828, *Glanthewenfeld, Glanthwenvell* 1554

W *llan* as above and ?saint *Llywenfel*; the poetry of Lewys Glyn Cothi (1447-89) records an oath *myn Llawenfel* which strengthens this suggestion. The pers.n. might contain W *llyw-* as in Llywel (below) or *llawen*, 'merry', and *mael*, 'chief, prince'. Modern sps. (from about the late 18thC) with *-lleonfel* have mixed up the vowels *o* and *e*. Theophilus Jones misinterpreted the pn. as 'Llan lleon voel, the church upon the bare tract' and says that the Roman road here was called *Sarn Lleon*, an error for Sarn Helen below. The 1554 sps. suggest confusion of *llan* with W *glan*, 'river-bank'.

## Llannerchygoedlan                                   SO 0940

*Llanhcoydelan* 1380, *Llanerch Coedlan* 1828, *Llanerch goedlan* 1832

'The coppice glade': W *llannerch*, 'clearing, glade', def.art. *y* and *coedlan*, 'copse, coppice'. A reputed manor. This may be *Llannerth Gydelach* 1566, probably a garbled sp.

## Llansanffraid (-ar-Wysg)                            SO 1223

*Lansefred* c.1100, 1321-2, *Lan San Fraid* 1140-50, *ll.san ffred* c.1566, *Llansanfrayd* 1578, *LLANSEYNTFREDE* 1535, (ch. of) *Sancta Brigida* 1254, *Brydecherch* 1310-11

This may also be (p. church of) *St. Mary de Sancto Brigida* 1476. 'Church of Sanffraid (Bride)', with *llan*. The prefix *San-, Sain(t)-*, 'saint, holy', is sometimes placed before the ns. of foreign saints, eg. *Seint y Katrin* (St. Catherine). Excluding extinct chapelries, there are 17 dedications to Sanffraid/Bride in Wales and about 30 in Brittany (as *Berc'het*). She may be a distinct saint from St. Brigid of Cill-muine in Ireland.

**Llansbyddyd, Llanspyddid**                    SO 0128

*Lamdespidic* 1127 (1374-7), *Landespetit* 1216, c.1291, *Lanespetit* 11thC (c.1200), *Lannspitit* c.1100, *LLAUNSPYDIT* 1405, *Llanspyddyd* 1832, *ll.ysbyðaid* c.1566, *Llanyspydyt* 13thC

W *llan* and a ?pers.n. *Ysbyddyd*, but no saint of this n. is known and the church is dedicated to Cadog (as in Llangatwg). Cadog, in his 'Life' c.1100, is said to have built a monastery here. Possibly a form of W *ysbyddaden*, pl. *ysbyddad*, *-aid* (note the c.1566 sp. above), now obsolete, meaning 'white thorn', as in *Pantysbyddyd* (lost, at SN 8831?) and *Tonysbyddaden* (SN 3612); a giant by the n. of *Ysbyddaden*, appears in the Mabinogi. The *-d-* in some sps. may be intrusive because W *llan* is sometimes found in AF sps. with *-d-* attached to it (cf. Llan-y-wern below) or the *-d-* may be the W prefix *ty-*, *dy-* placed before certain ns. as a mark of respect, particularly before the ns. of saints, eg. Llandysilio (Tysilio), Llandyfrydog (Tyfrydog) etc. There have been attempts to derive *Ysbyddyd* from w *ysbyty*, 'hospice, hospital', on the basis that the Priory of Malvern was connected with this locality, but this is very doubtful because of the dating.


**Llanthomas**                                  SO 2140

(half knight's fee) *Llan Thomas* 1504, 1522, (messuage) *Llanthomas* 1561, *LLANDTHOMAS* 1851, *Thomascherche* 1340

'Church of Thomas'; strictly speaking this ought to be *Llandomos*, *-domas* but we have not seen any sps. to confirm this form. The pn. may be quite a late creation deriving from a secular rather than the ecclesiastical *Thomas*. This was a chapel-of-ease to Llaneigon.


**Llanwrthwl**                                  SN 9763

*Lannochul* 1280, *Lanuchul* c.1291, *Llanuthull* 1559, early 17thC, *Llannothrill* 1421, *Llanwthwl* 1283, *LL.wrthwl* c.1550-62

'Church of Gwthwl', with *llan* as above and a pers.n., thought to be a saint, identified by some as *Gwrthmwl* (ModW *Gwrthfwl*), but the early sps. generally lack an -r- in -*wthwl*; on these grounds we can also reject *Gyrthmwl* or *Gwerthmwl Wledig* said in 'Englynion y Beddau' ('Stanzas of the Graves') to be buried in Celli Friafael near Pont-lliw GLA. The two first sps. above have the common scribal error of *c* for *t*.

**Llanwrtyd** SN 8647

**Llanwrtyd Wells** SN 8746
*Llanworted* 1554, *Llanurtid* 1553, *Llanurtyd* 1578, *Llanwrtid* 1596, *ll.wrtyd* c.1566, *LLanwrtyd Well* c.1778

'Church of ?Gwrtud' though the modern dedication is to Dewi/David. We cannot find any instances of *Gwrtud* as a pers.n. but it certainly appears to contain W *gŵr* and *tud*, 'sant gwryw' ('male saint'), according to Melville Richards, with *tud* as in *Tudglyd* and *Tudful*, 'daughters' of Brychan, *Tudwal*, and *Tudno* (the saint's n. in *Llandudno* CRN). There is nothing to support the suggestion that it has W *wrth y rhyd*, 'by the ford'!

The town of Llanwrtyd Wells developed after the discovery of a mineral well, traditionally by Rev. Theophilus Evans of Llangamarch in 1732, at a place called *Pont Rhydferan* c.1700, *Pont Rheed Vere* 1754, *Pontrhydvere, formerly a Meeting House* 1823, *Pont-rhyd-y-feri* 1833. This has W *pont*, 'bridge', and perhaps *berau, beri*, pl. of *bêr*, 'spear, lance', ?'fish-spear'; *berau, beri* would become *ferau, feri* [E pron. 'vereh, veree'] after *rhyd* which is a fem.n. The def.art. *y* in the 1833 sp. must be intrusive, a product of the *d* coming before the *v* sound.

**Llanynys** SN 9950
*Lanenus* c.1291, *Lanynys* 1374, *Lanynys in Buelt* 1395, *LLANYNYS* 1400, 1535, *ll.ynys* c.1566, *Llanynis* 1585, *Llanynnis Portheroyes* 1578, *Thlanvenys* 1361, *Llan Nonnys* 1547-51

W *llan*, 'church', and *ynys*, 'river-meadow' (as well as 'island'), as in the case of *Llanynys* DNB; it is not likely to contain the pers.n. ?*Mynys* as in Maesmynys (below). *Thlanvenys* seems to suggest that *Llanynys* may derive from *Llanfynys* (with loss of *-f-*) but it may well be a scribal error for *Thlannenys*. Moreover, the church dedication is to Llŷr not Mynys. The 1578 sp. has *Porthycrwys* shown on the 1832 OS map at SN 990497 as *Porth y crwys*, meaning 'gate near the crosses' with *porth*, 'gate, door' (and 'harbour'), def.art. and *crwys*, 'crosses'.

### Llan-y-wern SO 1028

*Landwern altera costinio* c.1100, *Londeworne* 1321-2, *Lanwern* c.1143-54, *Llanwerne* 1586, *ll. y wern mair a chynydr* c.1566, *Llan-y-wern* 1832, (hts.) *LLAN-Y-WERN, UPPER, ~, LOWER* 1804

W *llan* as above, def.art. *y* and *gwern*, 'alder-trees' elliptically 'place where alder-trees grow', which has developed the sense of 'wet, marshy land', i.e. 'church near a marsh'. The def.art. may have appeared later, an effect of the *-n-* before the vowel *-w-*: the small 'gap' which appears after the *-n-* may have been filled by a short, 'obscure' vowel (W *y*, pronounced very much like E *eh, uh*). The c.1566 sp. shows that the church was dedicated to Cynidr as well the present saint Mair/Mary.

Theophilus Jones identifies Llan-y-wern with Monkton which belonged to Brecon priory and occurs as (chp.) *Monkton* 1527, *Mounton* 1520-1, 1562. There is a farm here *Gwaunymynach* (SO 093298) which is *Gwaun y mynach* 1832: W *gwaun*, 'moorland, heath', def.art. *y* and *mynach*, 'monk'.

### Llech-faen SO 0828

*Leghvaine* 1593, *Llechfan* 1832, (ht.) *LLECHVANE* 1804, *Llechfan or Llanhamlech-fan* 1813, *Laghmane* 1310-11, *Laghmaen* 1311

W *llech*, 'slate', and *maen*, 'stone, large stone, rock', meaning perhaps 'flat or recumbent stone'; W *llechfaen* also occurs in the sense of 'slate, slab, flag, tablet'. In this pn. it seems to have become confused with *llechfan* composed of *llech* and *man*, loosely 'place'. A guide-book 1813 says that there was a ruinous chp. here which fell down in 1700, reputedly dedicated to Illtud, but this may well be 'Illtud's cairn'; see Llanhamlach. W *llech* also means 'a league' and indeed Llech-faen is about a league from Brecon but *llech* does not seem to appear in written sources before the 19thC. There is a *Pont Pentre-llech* (SN 9724) in Glyn and, in this particular instance, the likeliest meaning of *llech* may well be 'a league'.

**Llechryd**                                        SO 1009
(messuage) *Lechryd* 1770-9, (farms) *Upper and Lower Llechrydd* 1807

The area is called *Rumney bridge* 1814 and *Rumney Bridge* 1832 from the r. Rhymni which rises about a mile above Llechryd. Named from two farms Llechryd Uchaf and ~ Isaf ('upper', 'lower'), both referring to a ford, evidently preceding the bridge. W *llech* and *rhyd* would indicate 'stone ford, ford having stone slabs in it'. Formerly in BRE, transferred to MON in the late 19thC.

**Llechweddor** (lost: in Llanwrtyd)
*Llechweddol* 1823, (ht.) *LLECHWETHER* 1804

Probably W *llechwedd*, 'slope' etc.; the final part is likely to be a pl. *-or* as in *Croesor* MER, *Prysor* etc., and the whole might mean 'many slopes, hill area'. Final *-r* in W can sometimes be confused with *-l*; eg. E *corner* was borrowed as W *cornel*.

**Llwyncynog**                                      SO 0833
*Llwyncynog* 1828, *Llwyn-cynog* 1832, *Llwynynog* 1817

Melville Richards has *Llwyneurog* in his list but we have seen nothing to support this sp. W *llwyn*, 'bush, plant, grove', and pers.n. *Cynog* as in Llangynog above. One writer suggested *Llwyn-y-crog*, 'the bush of the cross' (with *crog*, 'cross, gallows'), but this does not fit the sps.

**Llwyn-onn Reservoir**                                          SO 0011

From the house (SO 013115), at the south end of the reservoir (opened 1927), called *Llwyn-on* 1832: 'ash-grove', with *llwyn* as above and *onn*, *ynn*, pl. of *onnen*, 'ash-tree'.

**Llyn y Fan Fawr** lake                                         SN 8321
*Llynyfan fawr*, *~ fach* 1814, *Llyn-y-fan-fawr* 1832, *Llyn Fawr* 1819

'Big lake of the peak': W *llyn*, 'lake, pool', def.art. *y* and *ban*, 'the peak', referring to *Fan Brycheiniog* (sic) (*Brecknock Van* 1831), the highest point of the Black Mountain. About 1½ miles west, at the foot of *Bannau Sir Gaer* ('peaks in CRM'), is *Llyn y Fan Fach* (SN 8021) CRM; this is the 'little lake near the peak'.

**Llysdinam**                                                    SO 0058
*Listinan* 1299, *Listivan (=Listinan)* 1291, *Lystynan* 1290, *Llestinan* 1578, *Llysdinam* 1672, 1756

W *llys*, 'court, palace' etc., and *dinan* (often pron. and spelt *dinam*), 'little stronghold'; *-d-* has provected or 'hardened' after the sibilant *-s-*. Llysdinam was apparently the administrative centre of Swydd Ddinan, one of the four sub-divisions (with Penbuellt, Swydd Dreflys and Swydd Irfon) of Buellt. This is *Southynan* 1360, *Swydhy vann* 1584 and occurs in (reeve of) *Inan* 1544-6. The last probably derives from a confused sp. of *de Dinan* misinterpreted as *de Inan*. *Dinan* occurs in *Dinam* (or *Dinham*) MON and in *Llandinam* MTG (with *llan*). Llysdinam was the home of Dafydd ap Maredudd in a poem of praise ('moliant') by Lewys Glyn Cothi 15thC and once possessed its own chp., ruinous in 1809.

**Llys-wen**                                                     SO 1337
*(Milo de) Lisewan* c.1127, *Liswen* 13thC, *LYSWEN* 1401, *y llyswen* c.1566, *Lyswen* 1388, *Leiswen* 1380, *Lyswen in Cantrecelly* 1443

'White court': W *llys*, 'court, palace, mansion-house' etc., and *gwen* fem of *gwyn*, 'white, fair' and 'holy'; there was also a man's pers.n. *Gwên* (with a long vowel pronounced rather like E *ehh*) but the sps. tend to support *gwen*. The pn. has inspired some extraordinary tales interpreting it as 'the gorgeous palace of the Princes of South Wales'. Local legend fixed the 'palace' in the Warren Field near Dderw.

**Llywel** SN 8630
(Saint) *Luhil* 12thC, *Luel* c.1200, 1210-12, 1372, *Luwel* 1295, *lli6uel* late 15thC, *Lhywel* 1584, *LLEWELL'* 1502, *Llowell'* 1326 (1516), *llan yn llywel* c.1180 (c.1400), (ch. of the three saints of) *Luel* 1239

Now a small village, a shadow of its 19thC extent, around a church dedicated to David/Dewi, a dedication confirmed in the poem 'Canu y Dewi' c.1180 by Gwynfardd Brycheiniog. In 1239 it is described as 'church of the three saints', thought to be David/Dewi, Teilo and either Padarn or (more likely) Llywel. As a saint *Llywel*, occurs in *Llanlowel* (properly *Llanllywel*) MON and probably *Lanlouel* in Brittany; he is reputed to have been a disciple of SS Dyfrig and Teilo. Some sps. such as *Iouguil, Iouhil, Iuhil, Iouguil* in the Book of Llan Dâv 12thC were thought by the scholar Baring-Gould to be earlier forms of *Llywel*, with a scribal error of *I-* for *L-*.

**Lower Chapel** see **Llanfihangel Fechan**

**Maes-car** SN 9428
*Maskar'* 1499, *Maiscar, -caro* 1536-9, *Maeskar* 1645, *Maes y Carr* 1756

Probably 'open land near r. Nant Car', with Aber-*car* (SN 929289) and Blaen-*car* (SN 932286) on its banks. This stream is one of three in BRE so named, but there are others, some unnamed, which probably contained the el. *car*; see Twyn Rhyd-car below. *Maes-car* is found in the farm n. and another called Beiliau Maes-car (misspelt *Bailea Maescar* on some OS maps). Maes-car is now the n. of a modern Community, earlier a p. and a hamlet; its antiquity suggests some other territorial unit.

### Maesgwarthaf                                    SO 2214
*Maes gwartha* 1624, *Maesgwartha* 1713, *MAESGWARTHA* 1804, *Maes-y-gwartha-ucha* 1832

'Uppermost field, uppermost open-land', with *maes* as above and *gwarthaf*.

### Maesmynys                                       SO 0249
*Maisminuth* 1280, *Maesmenus* c.1291, 1374, 1395, *MAYSMENYS in Buelt* 1491, *MAESMYNIS* 1804, *ll.ðewi maes mynys* c.1566

'Open land of Mynys' with *maes* as above and pers.n., not the n. of a saint – because the church is dedicated to Dewi/David, hence the c.1566 sp. standing for Llanddewi Maesmynys. There is very little evidence to suggest that Llanddewi was the leading n. of the p. as Melville Richards thought. There is an *Afon Mynys* (SN 7236-7231) near Llanwrda CRM.

### Malvern Llansbyddyd (lost)
*Llandespetit (Priorem . . . Malvernie)* 1223-5; (lp.) *Malverne Llanspythett* 1651

Following the conquest of BRE in the 12thC, the Anglo-Normans granted the church, tithes and land near the present village of Llansbyddyd to the priory of Malvern WOR which held it until the Dissolution.

### Manest hill                                      SO 1026
(hill) *Manest* 1815, (house) *Man-nest* 1832, *Mannest Isha, Cwm Mannest* 1739

Uncertain; similar pns. include *Manest* (at Coychurch) GLA and *Castell Manest* (Merthyr Cynog).

**Merthyr Cynog**                                          SN 9837

(grave of) *Kynauc in Merthyr Kynauc* 13thC, *Marteconot* 1127
(14thC), *MERTHERKONOK* 1502, *Merthir* c.1291, (rectory of)
*MARTHIRKENOCK* 1535, *Merthyrkynock* 1558, (church of) *Sĉi*
*CANOC* 1491

'Graveyard of Saint Cynog': W *merthyr* (from Lat *martyrium*)
meant 'grave of a saint, or churchyard consecrated with his
bones' as well as 'martyr'; similar ns., such as Merthyr Tudful,
have sometimes inspired extraordinary tales of a saint's
martyrdom. Similarly, Cynog (see also Llangynog), one of the
numerous 'sons' of Brychan Brycheiniog, was said by
Theophilus Jones to have been murdered by Saxons on the hill
Fanolau (*Vanoleu*) about two miles south-east of the church (at
SO 010359). Hugh Thomas c.1702, however, calls the site *the*
*Vann* which is likely to be the Fan (a hill at SN 9835) where
there is a prehistoric fort Corn-y-fan. There seems to have been
a well Ffynnon Gynog here. Thomas also records legends
associated with him by local people.

Cynog was certainly held in high respect and Merthyr Cynog
was a place of pilgrimage because the church possessed his
torque or collar, mentioned by Gerald of Wales c.1191 and Huw
Cae Llwyd late 15thC. There is also a mention of legends
associated with *Conoch* in 1538. Cynog had dedications
elsewhere at Battle, Defynnog, Llangynog, Ystradgynlais and
perhaps Llanganten, all in BRE, Bochrwyd (Boughrood) RAD,
Llangunnock MON, Llangunnock HER and possibly Llangynog
MTG.

**Modrydd**                                              SO 0025

*Modrith* 1372, 1693, *Modridd* 1715, *Modrydd* 1567, 1767, *Tyr*
*Modridd otherwise Holly Bush Hall* 1809

Obscure, but possibly a pers.n. containing the first el. found in
W *modrydaf*, 'chief, leader'. Today, the n. is used for a farm, but
earlier it was used for a hamlet of the p. of Llansbyddyd and a
civil p.

**Moel Feity** hill                                           SN 8422

*VOLE MITY* 1819, *Vole Vytte, Vytte Vechan* 1813, (hill) *Pen Foel*, (fms.) *Moity fawr, ~ isaf* 1814, *Moel-feudy* 1832

Presumably W *moel*, 'bald hill, bald mountain', but the remainder is uncertain, and the sps. are very late. The pn. evidently confused clerks. The modern sp. suggests *defeity*, literally 'sheep's house', 'sheep-cote' or 'farm where sheep are managed', ie. *Moel Ddefeity*, with loss of unstressed *Dde-*, producing *Moel 'Feity* but there are several farms here, viz. Meity Fawr, ~ Fechan and ~ Isaf called *Meu-dy-fawr, ~ -fechan, ~ -isaf* 1832, none having initial *F-* which is what one might expect if they were short forms of *Defeity*. It is possible that we actually have W *mei(dd)*, 'middle', thought to occur in W *meinoeth*, 'middle of the night', *Meifod* MTG (with *bod*, 'house', etc.), and *Meidrim* CRM (with *trum*, 'ridge, summit'), with *tŷ*, 'house', ie. 'middle house'. See Penmeiarth below. Sps. appear to rule out *meudwy*, 'hermit, anchorite', as a qualifier, ie. *Moel Feudwy*, though it seems to occur in *Ynysymeudwy* GLA.

**Monkton** see **Llan-y-wern**

**Mynydd Aberysgir** hill                                      SN 9932

*Mynydd Aber Esgair* 1817, *Mynydd Aberyscir* 1832

'Mountain in Aberysgir parish', with W *mynydd* and Aberysgir above.

**Mynydd Bwlch-y-groes** hill                                  SN 8634

*MYNYDD BWLCH-Y-GROES* 1832

'Mountain at the pass of the cross', with *mynydd* as above, *bwlch*, 'breach, gap, pass', def.art. and *croes*, 'cross' or, in this case, 'crossroads', probably that where mountain roads meet at the north end of the mountain (SN 8736). A house *Clydd-bwlch-y-groes* (*sic*) is shown at SN 874364 on the OS 1in. 1832; this appears as *Mountain Gate* 1734, which indicates that there was a 'gate' (W *clwyd*) here.

**Mynydd Epynt** hill                                       SN 9-4

*ipynt* 12thC, *Epyn* 1241, *gorwyt Epynt* c.1155-c.1195 (c.1400),
*epynt* c.1222 (early 14thC), *MYNYDD EPYNT* 1832, *Epint* 13thC,
*Eppint* 1623, *Eping Hill* 1798, *EPPINT HILLS* 1828, *Epyn* 1241

'Mountain with a horse-path', with *mynydd* as above and
probably *epynt*, composed of *eb*, 'horse' (as in *ebol*, 'foal') and
*hynt*, 'way', or perhaps a pers.n. *Epint* found in the Black Book
of Carmarthen 13thC. There are several ancient roads crossing
the mountain, notably that extending its length from SN 9140
past Tafarn-y-mynydd ('the mountain inn' at SN 918422),
Ffynnon David Bevan (SN 924429), Drover's Arms (*Drovers
Tavern* 1828, *Pen-y-gefn-ffordd* 1833, 'top of the ridge-way', (SN
986452) to SN 034457. This may be that called *Y genffordd ar
Eppint* 1623, *Kevenforth ar Epint* 1653, 'the ridgeway on Epynt'.

**Mynydd Illtud** hill see **Capel Illtud**

**Mynydd Llangatwg** hill                                  SO 1814

'Mountain in Llangatwg p., mountain part of Llangatwg'. The
south-east part Mynydd Pen-cyrn is called *MYNYDD PEN
CYRN* 1832 probably having *pen* and either *curn*, pl. of *cyrnen*,
'cone, stack', or *curn*, *cyrn*, 'heap, mound; cone, stack' (see
Gurnos above). The centre of the hill is *Twr pen-cyrn*, 'Pen-cyrn
heap', where there are several cairns. *Mynydd Pen-cyrn* seems to
mean roughly 'mountain with a summit marked by stacks'.

**Mynydd Llan-gors** hill                                  SO 1627
*Cocket Hill* 1816-17, *Mynydd Llangorse* 1832

'Mountain in Llan-gors parish'. *Cockit Hill* is now applied solely
to the north part of the mountain adjoining the pass called
*Cockit* 1816-17 (SO 160284) and *the Cockit* 1773-78. The n. *Cocket*
is applied to a house or farm on the OS 1in. map 1832. Similar
pns. occur elsewhere: Cockett (W *Y Cocyd*), in Swansea, occurs

as *le Cockett* 1583, *the Cockett* 1650, *Cocked* 1670 and *Cockit* 1799 and there is an example of a tenement called *ye Gockett* 1670 at Pentyrch GLA. Neither has been satisfactorily explained though they might contain E *cock* in the sense 'hay-cock': perhaps 'hill shaped like a hay-cock'.

**Mynydd Llangynidr** hill                                     SO 1214
*MYNYDD LLANGYNIDR* 1832

'Mountain in Llangynidr p., mountain part of Llangynidr'. Called *Tir Foel Glas* 1814 but see Trefil below.

**Mynydd Llysiau** hill                                       SO 2027
*Mynydd Llysiau* 1832

'Mountain characterised by vegetables or herbs', with *mynydd* as above and *llysau, llysiau*. Just to the north is another hill *Pen Trumau*, 'ridges' top'. A path descending its west side is called *Rhiw Trumau* (*Rhiw trumau* 1832), 'ridges slope'

**Mynydd Pen-y-fâl** hill                                     SO 2619
*MYNYDD PEN-Y-FÂL* 1832, *Pen y vale Hill* 1695, (hill) *Penvayle* 1612, *Penyvale Hills* 1805

Now shown as the north spur of the Sugar Loaf (SO 2718) but in 1832 it is applied to the entire mountain and *SUGAR LOAF* is applied to the portion just inside MON and it is very likely that they are simply alternative W and E ns. for the same mountain. *Sugar Loaf* (*Sugar Loaf* 1806, ~ *Hill* 1828) must refer to its shape; the n. is fairly common in England and there is another *Sugar Loaf* (SN 8342) in Llanfair-ar-y-bryn CRM. *Pen-y-fâl* has W *pen*, 'head, top', def.art. *y* and *bâl*, 'peak, summit'; the poet Drayton 1612 (ref. above) says 'so named of his bald head'!, ie. *moel*, 'bald, bald hill'.

**Mynydd Trawsnant** hill                                    SN 8248
*Mynydd Trawsnant* 1833

'Mountain near Trawsnant (fm.)' which is *Trawsnant* 1820-1
with W *traws*, 'across, over' and *nant*, probably in the sense of
'area around a stream or streams'.

**Mynydd Troed** hill                                    SO 1629, 1728
*Mynyd Trod* 1574, *Mynydd Troed* 1816-17, 1832

W *mynydd* as above and *troed* (often pron. *trôd* in south Wales
rhyming with E 'road'), 'foot': 'mountain shaped like a foot' or
perhaps 'foot-hill of the Black Mountains'.

**Mynydd y Glog** hill                                    SN 9808
*Mynydd y Glogue* 1840, *Glog Hills* 1819

W *mynydd*, 'mountain, moorland', and *clog* (*glog* after the
def.art. *y*), 'rock, cliff', describing this rock-strewn upland
moorland. At its western end there is a hillock Twyn y Glog
(*twyn*, 'hillock, knoll') and on its slope there was a farm (SN
955087), called *Gloge* 1814, abandoned due to quarrying. At its
eastern end there is Pen-moel-allt which occurs as *MYNYDD
PENMAILARD* 1814, *Mynydd Penmailard*, (house) *Penmailard*
(SN 013094) 1832. Dewi Cynon (*Hanes Plwyf Penderyn*) says that
local people called this *Penmeulart* which he regarded as a
corruption but it might have W *meilart*, 'drake', and *pen*, 'head',
used in a topographical fashion like Penderyn ('bird's head')
below.

**Nant-ddu** (Capel Nant-ddu)                                    SO 0014
*Capel Nantye* 1578, *Cappel Nantee* 1548, *Capell Nant ddu* 1798,
*Nant ddu Chapel* 1813, (hamlet) *Nantdu* c.1670

'Black, dark stream', with W *nant* and *du*; *nant* was earlier
regarded as masc. giving *du* (without a mutation), later as fem.
with *du* mutating as *ddu*. Sps. of this n. with *ddu* tend to be later.

The r. rises near the mountain Craig Fan-ddu (SO 018184). There was a chapel-of-ease here (to Cantref) but it was demolished in 1998.

### Nantyrarian SO 0350

*Nant-yr-Arrian* 1828, *Nant-yr-arian* 1832

'Stream of silver, silvery stream'?: W *nant*, 'stream' (earlier 'valley'), def.art. *yr* and *arian, ariant,* 'silver, money'. The last is a common el. in rns., eg. *Nantyrarian* (SN 7181), a tributary of Melindwr, CRD. The r. reaches the r. Irfon at SO 032506.

### Nedd, Neath rn.

*Need* c.1100, *Ned* c.1150, *Neth* 1191, 1372, *Nethe vaghan* 1502-3, *Neeth* 1306, *Neath flu:, Neath vachan flu:* 1578, *Neath* 1602

Richards favoured 'shining r.' containing Brit root *\*nid-*, possibly related to Lat *nideo,* 'to shine'. Nedd Fechan has W *bechan,* mutated as *Fechan,* 'little, lesser'.

### Neuadd Reservoirs SO 0218

Two small reservoirs on the upper reaches of the r. Taf Fechan, named after Neuadd Fach (*Neuadd-fach* 1832 at SO 030186). W *neuadd,* 'hall', is a very common n. for large houses and farmhouses; with *bach,* mutated as *Fach,* 'small, lesser'.

### Newchurch see Tirabad

### Newton: Y Drenewydd, SO 034287
Llan-faes
*Neweton* 1281,(church) *Neweton* 1373, *Niweton* 1309, *Neuton* 1290, *Y dref newydd* 1534-80, *Trenewith* 1536-9, 1600-7, *NEWTON, alias ST. DAVID'S, UPPER DIVISION* 1804, *Newton* 1832, *NEWTOUN* 1326 (1516)

'New farm or settlement': ME *niwe, new* and *-ton* (from OE *tūn*). The site of a house built 1582 by Sir John Games, described by Hugh Thomas as 'one of the fairest in the County' 1698. 'New settlement' perhaps in contrast to the older site of Llan-faes.

**Newton**                                              SO 1124
Llansanffraid
*Newtown* 1814, *Newton* 1832, *la Neuton* (in manor of Talgarth) 1309, *Newton Llansanfred* 1630

This may also be *Neweton* 1373. As Newton (Llan-faes) but the sps. are later; reputedly the birthplace of the poet Henry Vaughan (1622-95). Formerly 'a fine mansion . . . now a farmhouse' (Poole 1886).

**Pant Sychbant** valley                                SN 9809
*Sych-pant* 1832

'Dry hollow', with *sych*, 'dry, parched', and *pant*, 'hollow, depression', which mutates after the qualifier *sych*. This n. describes an area characterised by limestone sinks where the r. Nant Cadlan flows west and disappears into Ogof Fawr, 'big cave', The addition of *pant* at the beginning of the n. appears to be superfluous but similar repetitions are found in other W pns. The n. is also found in the ns. of farms recorded as *Sych-pant-isaf*, ~ *-uchaf* 1832, *Sychpantisaf*, ~ *-uchaf* 1814 (SO 0010), which take their ns. from a stream Nant Sychbant which rises on Pant Sychbant but flows eastwards.

**Patrisio, Partrishow**                                SO 2722
*Merthyr Issui* 12thC, *pertrissw* c.1566, *Patryssowe* 1556-8, *PATRISHOW* 1804, *Patricio* 1828, *Partricio* 1832, *Llanysho* 1555

The church is dedicated to *Isio*, given by some as *Issui* and variants *Isw, Ishaw, Isho*, and there is a *St. Isho's Well* alias *Ffynnon Ishow* recorded by Richard Fenton. The pn. has excited a great deal of misinterpretation, eg. Archdeacon Payne 1806 suggested a derivation from *'Parthau'r Ishew* – the Parts, or District of Ishew'.

The correct sp. of the saint's n. is uncertain because of the paucity of early sps. but the first el. is W *merthyr*, as in Merthyr Cynog above and other pns. such as Merthyr Tudful and Merthyr Mawr (properly Merthyr *Myfor*) GLA, meaning not 'martyr' (giving rise to the story of Issui being murdered by a traveller) but 'grave of a saint or churchyard consecrated with his bones'. The modern sps. with *P*- may have developed from *Merthyr Isio* being reconstructed unconsciously as *Perth'risio*; to say 'I live in Merthyr Isio' and 'I live in Perth'risio', W speakers might say 'Rwy'n byw ym Merthyr Isio' and 'Rwy'n byw ym Mherth'risio' – sufficiently close for the difference to be overlooked. Over a long period of time the *M*- and the *P*- might be confused and *Merthyr Isio* forgotten as the original form. The sps. with *Pat*- may be explained as shortenings of *Perth*-, *Pert*- because the stress lay on the 'ish' of *-isio*.

### Pen-allt                                                          SO 1917
*PENALT* 1804, (farms) *Pen-allt-isaf*, ~ *-uchaf* 1832, *Penallt*, ~ *isaf* 1816-17

Perhaps 'hill with a wooded slope', with *pen*, 'head, height, hill', and *allt* as in Allt-mawr above.

### Pen Allt Mawr hill                                              SO 2024
*Pen-allt-mawr* 1832

It is difficult to be certain because sps. are few and 'late' and because there is no mutation after *allt* (*mawr* to *fawr*) which is usually a fem. n. (as in Allt Ddu above). It would appear to mean 'hill near a wooded slope' but is it properly *Penallt Mawr*, 'big Penallt (top of wooded slope)' as opposed to some lost hill called *Penallt-bach*, 'little Penallt'? *Allt* itself may have replaced some word such as *garth*.

**Pen-buallt**                                    SN 9244
*Penbelth* 1360, *Penbuelth* 1424-5, *Pennebuelth* 1544-6, 1550,
*Penbuallt* 1553-8, *PENBYALT* 1804, *llys penn* c.1566

'Top end or upland of Buellt', a former t. of Llangamarch p. and
a *swydd* (see Treflys and Swydd Irfon) at the west end of the
cantref of Buellt (see Builth above). The c.1566 ref. has W *llys*,
'court, hall', possibly the site of the administration of this area.


**Pencelli**                                      SO 0925
(castle) *Penkelly* 1233 (late 13thC), 1377-8, *castell Pen Kelli* 1215
(c.1400), (castle of) *Penkelli* 1233 (c.1286), *Pencelhy* 1584, *Penkethly*
1310-11, *Penkethlyn* 1373, *Penkelthyn* 1313, *Penkerlyn in commoto
de Tyrrauf* 1294, *P(enkelly) Anglican*, ~ *Wallens* 1521-2, *Penkellye
Wallenses alias ye Welche Penkelly* 1651

Probably 'end of grove', with *pen* in the sense of 'end of' and
*celli*, 'grove, copse, woodland'. This was the n. of a lp., probably
taking its n. from its main castle. The lp. was divided into the
manors of *Pencelli Castle, English Pencelli, Welsh Pencelli* (named
above), *Pencelli Cwmorgwm, Wenallt, Pencelli Glyncollwng* and
*Cwmbanw*. The castle possessed a chp. of St. Leonard recorded
in 1502. See also Tir Ralff for the 1294 ref. above.


**Pen Cerrig Calch** hill                          SO 2122
*Pen-cerrig-calch* 1832

'Limestones hill', with *cerrig*, pl. of *carreg*, 'stone, rock', and
*calch*, 'lime'. Payne 1806 calls it *the Breannog Mountain* and its
summit *Cefn-digell* while Greenwood's map 1828 distinguishes
*Briannog Hill* and *Cefn-digell*. *Breannog* is evidently the modern
OS map's *Bryniog* (SO 1922), a n. confined to the spur about a
mile west of Pen Cerrig-calch. The correct form of *Bryniog* is
uncertain: *bryniog* is an adj. meaning 'hilly', implying a lost n.,
perhaps *mynydd* to match Payne's *Mountain* but 'hilly
mountain' would seem a little odd. Perhaps *bryniog* has
replaced *breannog* through popular interpretation; is *breannog* an

adj. (*breuannog*?) formed from *breuan*, 'handmill, quern, mill-stone' ?

**Penderyn**     SN 9408
*Penederyn* 1372, *PENNEDERYN* 1493, *PENNEDERYNE* 1410, *Penyderyn* 1513, *Pennyderyn* 1291, 1376, *Penhederyn* 1559, *Penderin* 1373, *Penderyn* 1522, (ch. of) *Spemederm* 1282

Literally, 'bird's head', with *pen* and *aderyn, ederyn,* 'bird', probably referring to some topographical feature such as Foel Penderyn (SN 935087). R.J. Thomas suggested that it might preserve the memory of animal sacrifice and others have suggested that the n. is totemistic, ie. the head of a particular animal might be set on a pole, marking a site of assembly (see CVPN, pp.76-78). There are similar ns., eg. *Penarth* MTG and GLA, 'bear's head', and *Pentyrch* GLA, 'boars' head', but topographical features might explain most if not all. There is no evidence to suggest that *Penderyn* contains W *tarren,* 'knoll, rock', as Theophilus Jones thought. Other impossible suggestions have included *Penderwen,* 'oak-tree head or hill', and *Pen-dau-ryn,* 'head of two ridges'. The 1282 form is a remarkable misspelling; the two letters *m* are likely to be scribal errors for *n* or *nn* and *in*. The letters *m, ni, in, u* and *n* are often confused by medieval clerks.

**Pen Gwyllt Meirch** hill     SO 2425
*Pen-gwellt-march* 1832, *Pengallt March* 1816-17

The evidence is insufficient: the modern form suggests *pen*, probably in the sense of 'hill' (a common meaning in this area), *gwyllt,* 'wild', and *meirch,* 'horses', although one might have expected *Gwyllt-feirch* with a mut. after the adj. *gwyllt*. The 1832 sp. makes better grammar: with *gwellt,* 'grass', and *march,* 'horse, stallion', in the sense of 'hill where there was suitable grass for horses'. *March* is sometimes employed to mean 'coarse' just as E *horse* is used in 'horse-radish', but in that case it generally precedes its noun.

**Penmeiarth, Penmyarth**                    SO 1820
*Pennmyarth* 1638, *Pen myerdd* 1813, *PEN MYARTH* 1811,
(common) *Myarth* 1612-35, (hill) *Mayarch* (for *Mayarth*) c.1234-
40, *Mayhard* c.1234, *Miarth* 1832, *Fforest Myarth*, ~ *Meyarth* 1561

'Middle ridge', with *mei(dd)* (found also in *Meifod* MTG and
*Meidrim* CRM) and *garth*, 'mountain-ridge, promontory'.
*Penmeiarth* is also the n. of the house at its east end (*pen*, 'head,
end') and the n. of a manor.

**Pen Milan** hill                           SN 9923
*Pen milan* 1814, *Pen-milan* 1832

The sps. are really too late: presumably W *pen*, 'hill' etc., but the
second el. is uncertain unless it is from W *milain*, 'villein,
peasant', possibly used as an adj. to mean 'cruel, rough, hard'.
Greenwood's map 1828 shows *Green Hill* here, evidently a
corruption of *Y Gyrn*, the hill about a mile to the south.

**Pen-pont, Betws Pen-pont**                 SN 9728
*Penpont* 1223-5, *Penponte* 1536, *Tire Penpont* 1586, *Penbont* 1531,
*Bettws, or Penpont Chapel* 1815, *Penpont, Capel Bettws* 1798

'Bridge end', with *pen*, in the sense of 'end of', and *pont*. The
church here, a former chapel-of-ease to Llansbyddyd, is Betws
Pen-pont with W *betws*, 'chapel, bead-house', named as *Capel
Bettws* 1798 and 1832, a rather odd tautology. The bridge over
the r. Usk is said to have been built c.1670 but the earlier sps.
prove that there was a much older bridge here. The chp. was
ruinous in 1728 and was re-built c.1789 and 1865. Pen-pont is
best known for its mansion constructed for Daniel Williams
c.1666.

**Pen-rhos**                                 SN 8011

'End of moor', with *pen* and *rhos*, 'moor' (as well as
'promontory'). A late 19thC development serving the nearby

coal mine taking its n. from a farm which is *Penrhose* 1729, 1819, 1829.

**Pentre-bach**                                                 SN 9032
*Pentre-bach* 1832

'Little village': W *pentre(f)* and *bach*, 'little, lesser', very likely in contrast to Pentre'r-felin about two miles lower down the valley of the r. Cilieni.

**Pentre Dolau-honddu**                                         SN 9943
*Pentre Dolhonddu* c.1817, *Pentre-dolau-honddu* 1832

'Village in meadows by the r. Honddu': *pentre(f)* as above, *dolau*, pl. of *dôl*, 'meadow, dole, field'; for the r. *Honddu*, see Brecon above.

**Pentre'r-felin**                                              SN 9130
*Pentreyr Velin* 1754, *Pentre-felin* 1832

'The mill village': *pentre(f)*, def.art. *y* attached to the *-e* as '*r* and *melin*, 'mill'. *Melin* is fem. and mutates after the def.art. to produce *Felin*. The site of a mill over the r. Cilieni.

**Pentwyn Reservoir**                                           SO 0515

Named from the farm *Pen-twyn* 1814, 1832 which stood near the dam: *pen* and *twyn*: 'end of hillock'. The 'hillock' may be *Twyn-disgwylfa* (SO 0414): *Twyn Disgwylva* 1828, *Twyn-disgwylfa* 1832, now unnamed on maps: 'look-out place'.

**Pen-y-cae**                                                   SN 8413
*Pen-y-cae* 1819, 1829

'Head or top of the field'. Today's village takes the n. of one of its earliest houses given as *Pen-y-cae house and garden* on the 1844 tithe map. The south end of the village is the former farm shown as *Pontrhydarw*, ~ *Ffarm* 1814, *Pont-rhyd-arw* 1832; *Pont-*

*rhyd-arw* is 'bridge at rough ford': W *pont*, 'bridge', *rhyd*, 'ford', and *garw*, mutated as *arw*, 'rough, coarse'.

**Pen-y-crug** antiquity                                    SO 0230
*Pen y Kreeg* c.1700, *Pen y Krug* 1705 ,(fms.) *Penycrug-uchaf*, *Penycrugisaf* 1817, *Pen-y-crug* 1832

Probably 'hill characterised by a heap or mound': W *pen*, def.art. *y* and *crug*, 'hillock, knoll; cairn; heap' etc. referring, no doubt, to the hill-fort here. The n. is also borne by the farm *Pen-crug* (= *Penycrug-uchaf* 1817).

**Pen y Manllwyn** hill                                    SO 2031
*Pen y manllwyn* 1832, *Mannllwdn* 1816-17

W *pen* in its sense of 'hill', def.art. and *manllwdn*, *mân llwdn*, 'a sheep, ?ewe; small animal; mutton' according to GPC, confused with *mân*, 'small, little', and *llwyn*, 'grove', etc.

**Peutyn**                                    SO 0431
*Peytevenescastel* 1373, *Petevenescastell* 1522, *y pevtyn* c.1550-62, *ar peutun*, *Yny peutun* late 15thC, *Pityn* 1600-7, *Pytin Gwyn*, *Pytinduy* 1783, *Peytyn-glâs*, ~ *-du*, ~ *-gwyn* 1832, *Payton* 1559

A manor. Hugh Thomas 1698 spells it *Poitins* and says that a Sir Richard Poitins acquired it from Bernard de Neufmarché late 11thC and Theophilus Jones and Poole add that the manor was purchased by Llywelyn, father of Sir Dafydd Gam (d. 1415), from William Peyton. The n. is now borne by three farms distinguished as *glas*, 'green' (and 'blue'), *gwyn*, 'white', and *du*, 'black', possibly referring to the colour of their soil or vegetation. Sir Richard Poitins appears to be unrecorded elsewhere but the pn. certainly contains a genuine surname spelt variously *Poidevin*, *Podevin*, *Poitevin*, *Peitevyn*, 'a man from Poitou' (DES). We know that a certain Philip *Peytevin* held half-a-fee in the lp. of Brecknock 1299, possibly at Peutyn. The mentions of a castle are interesting since there is none known here apart from that in Llanddew. We know also that there was a manorial fee called *Peitevin* 12thC and *Peittevin* late 13thC in Kenfig GLA.

### Pipton
SO 1638

*Piperton* late 12thC, *Pipertone* 1321, *Pipurton* 1380, *Pipeton by Langoyt* 1373, *Pipton alias Peperton* 1722, *Pipton* 1578

Either an OE pers.n. *Pippra, Pippa* as in Peppering SSX or OE *pipere*, 'piper', as a surname or epithet, with ME *-ton*. There is no need to look for an Anglo-Saxon outpost here (as M.L. Dawson); it probably belongs to the period after the conquest of Brycheiniog by Bernard de Neufmarché. Bernard is known to have granted Glasbury church to the abbey of St. Peter's, Gloucester, in 1088. A chaplain of *Piperton* is recorded in the late 12thC and there was a chp. here, mentioned in 1754 and 1798; it was in ruins in 1811.

### Ponde
SO 1037

*Melin-pandy, Pandy* c.1817, *Melin Pandy, Pandy* 1832

Apparently, W *pandy*, 'fulling-mill, tucking-mill', but the modern sp. suggests '(mill) pond', and more sps. are needed to resolve the matter. There is a reference to *Pownde y Velin* 1524 which may be here; this appears to have W *pownd*, 'pound' def.art. *y* and *melin*, 'mill', and it is possible that *Ponde* derives from this sp. rather than *pandy*.

### Pont-faen
SN 9934

*Pontfaen* 1817, *Pont-faen* 1832

'Stone bridge', with *pont*, 'bridge', and *maen*, 'stone, esp. one having some speciality or a particular use' and used as qualifier. The pn. is fairly common, eg. *Pontfaen* PEM and *Y Bont-faen* (= Cowbridge) GLA.

**Pontneddfechan**                                    SN 9007
*Pontneath Vaughan Farm* 1798, *Pontneathvaughan* 1815, 1828, *pont neath vechan* 1691, *Pont-nedd-fechan* 1832

'Bridge over lesser r. Nedd/Neath'. The modern sp. with *-vaughan* seems to have been a product of E speakers associating *Fechan*, 'lesser, junior', with the W surname *Vaughan* which itself derives from the masc. form *Fychan*.

**Pontsenni** see **Sennybridge**

**Pontsticill**                                       SO 0511
*Pont Stickel* 1729, *Pontsticell* 1814, *Pont-sticill* 1832, *Pontstickill Farm* c.1825, *Pont-y-stickyll, a bridge of one arch* 1807

'Stile bridge': W *pont* and *sticill*, a word borrowed from OE *stigel*, 'stile'. Also the n. of a reservoir otherwise called Taf Fechan Reservoir.

**Pontwilym**                                         SO 0430
*le Ponte Willym* 1536-7, *Pont 6ilym* late 15thC, *Pontwillim* 1698, *Pont-gwilym* 1832, (Thomas Havard of) *Port Will'm* 1569

'Gwilym's bridge', with W *pont* and *Gwilym*, mutated as *-wilym* because *pont* is a fem. n. *Gwilym* is a borrowing from ME *William*.

**Pont-y-wal**                                        SO 1335
*Pountewal, --walle* 1380, *Pontewall* 1522, *Pontywall* 1585, *Pont-y-wall* 1817, *PONTWALL* 1599, *Pontwall in Cantreselly* 1443

Probably W *pont*, def.art. *y* and *gwal*, 'wall': 'the wall bridge, bridge with walls'.

**Pool**                                              SO 0130
*Poole* 1558, 1535, (grange) *the Poole* 1527, (manor) *Pool* 1530, *Pool* 1817

Probably ME *pool* derived from OE *pōl, pull*, 'pool', but the present farm has no pool; the nearest is at *Pysgodlyn* (SO 021307) some distance away, meaning 'fish-pool, fish-pond', with W *pysgod*, 'fish', and *llyn*, 'lake, pool'. The pn. might derive from a surname and in Crucadarn there was a *Pool Hall*, now Y Neuadd (SO 9842), built by (and commemorating) Howel *Powell* in the 17thC,

### Porthamal                                                    SO 1635
*Porthamal, i.e. Porta Copiae* 1536-9, *Porthamall* 1602, *Porthammell* 1572, *Porthamble* 1578, *Porthamball* 1574, *Parthanell, Porthamell* 1559, *Porthanvill, -anul* 1380

The first ref. is taken from John Leland's *Itinerary* 1536-9, his Latin meaning 'many gates', matching the W *porth*, 'gate, door', and *aml*, 'frequent' (loosely perhaps 'large'); the whole referring to the large gatehouse of Great Porthamal or elliptically to the large, important house itself. The pn. has also been translated as 'many Portals' (but *porth* is sing. not pl.) and as 'the portal of plenty'. There is a farm at Nantmel RAD called *Porthamel* 1869 but *Porthaml* (*Porthamal* 1294) ANG is thought to have an Ir pers.n. *Amal*.

### Pwll-y-wrach                                                 SO 1732
(ht.) *PWLL-Y-WRAEH* 1804, *Pwll-y-wrach* 1778, 1832

'The witch's pool', with *pwll*, 'pool, pit', def.art. *y* and *gwrach* (mutated after the def.art.), 'hag, witch'. The n. is now used for a nature reserve which contains a pool above the waterfall on the r. Enig (properly Brennig) which runs from Mynydd Bychan through Talgarth.

### Rhiwbenmynydd (lost)                                         ?SO 060326
(Grant of free warren in) *Ryopenmenith* 1281, (grant of market and fair at) *Rubenmennith* 1290

'Slope at a mountain-top': *rhiw*, 'slope, ascent', *pen*, 'head, hill' etc., and *mynydd*, 'mountain'. Its location is uncertain; William

Rees placed it near Porth-gwyn (location above). There is a farm *Rachfynydd* (*Rhach-fynydd* 1832) (at SO 046320) about one mile south of Porth-gwyn.

**Rhiwiau**                                                    SO 0839
*Rue* 1380, *Rhywe* 1617, *Rhiwau* 1832

'Slopes': W *rhiwiau*, pl. of *rhiw*; in most of south Wales the pl. ending is pron. *-e* or *-a*, hence the sps. for 1380 and 1617.

**Rhosferig**                                                  SO 0152
*Rhosverig* 1754, *Rhosferig* 1813, (hamlet) *RHOSFERRIG* 1804, *Rhosferrik Court or Llacha and Tirinow . . . now called Rhosferrig* 1801

*Keuenrosuerek* occurs hereabouts 1278. W *rhos*, 'moor', and perhaps *merig*, a hypothetical adj. based on W *mêr*, 'marrow', meaning 'moor abounding with marrows'? Sps. make the pers.n. *Meurig* unlikely. The 1278 sp. has W *cefn*, 'back, ridge'.

**Rhyd-briw** see **Capel Rhyd-briw**

**Rhymni** rn.

*Remni* 1101-20, *Remny* 12thC, *Rempny* 1401, *Glynrempny* 1313-14, *Reempni* 13thC, *Rympni avon* 1072 (14thC), *Rompney* 1610, *avon Rymhi* 1069 (late 13thC), *Blaen ~, Duffrin Rumney* 1798, *Blaen Rumney, Lowr. Rumney, Rumney Uppr. Furnace* 1832

R.J. Thomas suggests *rhwmp*, 'auger, gimlet', comparable with the r. Taradr, meaning much the same, but the *-p-* seems to be a later intrusion. There are similar rns. elsewhere such as in *Blaen-rhymni* near Pontardawe GLA, *Rummy* (SO 049680) RAD and *Close Romny* 1536 near Llansanffraid BRE. The industrial town Rhymney MON about two miles downriver from the old border of BRE and MON developed after the establishment of ironworks by the 2nd Marquess of Bute in the 1820s, shown as *Bute Iron Works* and *Rumney Iron Works* on the OS 1in. 1832.

### Saint Eiliwedd (at Slwch) ?SO 056285

*S'aueleh* 1200-30, *Sancte Aissilde* 1147-56, *Sancte Haellilde* 1115-47, *sancte Elivehe* 1411-12, *Sancta Eleveta* 1459-61, *sanctam Elvetam* 1454, *St. Eylet* 1527, *St. Alice* 1509-47, *St. Arbete* 1550, *St. Arbeta's chapel* 1577

This may be *Lanhuleth* 1372, *Lanhewleth* 1454. Gerald of Wales mentions the church of *Sanctæ Aelivedhæ* c.1191 on the summit of a hill, the site of her martyrdom, not far from the castle of Brecon. The saint's n. must have been particularly perplexing – to judge by the sps. above – to scribes and antiquarians. Theophilus Jones himself calls her variously *Elud, Alud, Elyned* and *Aluned*. According to Hugh Thomas local people associated the chp. with *St. Taylad*. She is almost certainly *Eiliwedd*, yet another 'daughter' of Brychan Brycheiniog, appearing in a manuscript c.1200; the pers.n. may be composed of W *eiliw*, 'face', and *gwedd*, 'appearance, form' (ETG p. 157).

The chp. (*St. Elyned's Chapel* on the OS 2½ in. scale map 1952) seems to have stood at the foot of the hill Slwch Tump at the top of Cerrigcochion Lane which is called *St. Ellan Layne* in accounts of Brecon priory 1536-7. The 1387 ref. describes a lane – apparently an extension to *St. Ellan Layne* – running *from the stone bridge over the Hotheney* [Upper Bridge?] *towards Saint Kaleth*. The chp. lacked tiles in 1698 and is thought to have fallen down soon afterwards.

### Saint John the Evangelist, Brecon SO 044290

(ch. of) *Sancti Johannis de Brechonia* c.1150-75, *Sancti Johannis Evangeliste de Brechonia* c.1240-47, *St. Johns in town of Brecon* 1572, *aberhodni: ifan fedyðiowr* c.1566

Thought to have been founded c.1093-5 by Bernard de Neufmarché, serving both the priory and p. Dedicated to John the Evangelist (John, 'the Divine') according to most sources but the W source c.1566 above gives it as John the Baptist. This has *Ifan* (or *Ieuan, Ioan*) and *Bedyddiwr*, mutated as *Fedyddiwr*. The church had a chp. of St. Lawrence recorded in 1527 and a St. Keyne's chp.

**Saint Mary, Brecon**                                    SO 045285

(church of) *Sancte Marie de Brechonia* c.1215, *a mighti great chapel (S. Mariae)* 1536-9, *S. Marys ward* 1610

Dedicated to Mary a former Benedictine priory church and chapel-of-ease to Saint John the Evangelist. Now the cathedral church of the diocese of Swansea and Brecon.

**Sarn Helen** Roman road                                 SN 9013,9217

*Sarn Helen, Roman Road* 1832

The n. may once have applied to the whole of the Roman road from Y Gaer (Brecon) to Neath GLA. The n. is given to Roman roads elsewhere in Wales, including that running from Y Gaer (Forden) through Newtown to Caersws MTG (*surne Ellen* 1627); the north-south road through Tomen-y-mur Roman fort MER and northwards through Ffestiniog and Penmachno CRN; the road running south from Trawsgoed Roman fort CRD; and the road running south from Caerau (SN 9250) BRE. Early refs. to these roads are very scarce. Traditionally, they were made by Helen, wife of the Emperor Magnus Maximus and mother of Constantine, and it is possible that some native *Elen* has been confused with her. In 'The Dream of Maxen' in the Mabinogion it is said that Elen of the Hosts 'thought to make high roads from one stronghold to another across the Island of Britain . . . And for that reason they are called the Roads of Elen of the Hosts . . . ' It is quite possible that the tales associated with these roads are onomastic, i.e. an original *sarn halen* or 'salt road' has been interpreted as *Sarn Elen* and a mythical Elen or Helen has been invented to explain the n.

**Scethrog** see **Sgethrog**

**Sclydach** see **Ysclydach**

**Senni** rn. see **Capel Senni**

**Sennybridge: Pontsenni**                    SN 9228
*Senny Bridge* 1829, *Senni Bridge* 1833

A village which developed around a bridge (W *pont*)
constructed c.1819 to take the new mailcoach road over the r.
Senni. Further development resulted from the building of the
terminus and depôt of the Brecon Forest Tramroad 1820-30 but
its most significant development took place after the
construction of the Neath & Brecon Railway 1872. The present
house Pen-y-bont (SN 925286), about half-a-mile from the
bridge, appears at that time when the original Pen-y-bont (SN
925290) became the stationmaster's house.

**Sgethrog, Scethrog**                    SO 1025
*Skadroc* 1215-22, *Skatherok* 1373, *Scatheroc* 1254, *Scathorock* 1310-
11, *Skatherogg* 1583, *Skathrok* early 13thC, *Skethrog* 1578,
*Yskethrog* 1698

Melville Richards favoured W *ysgathrog*, with a later dialect
version *ysgethrog*, 'scattered (place)', and comparable with
*gwasgardir*, 'dispersed land', found in Bangor and Llandygái
CRN. Perhaps 'scattered settlement'. Attempts to derive it from
W *ysgithrog*, are unconvincing in view of the sps. with *Ska-*, *Ske-*;
*ysgithrog* can mean 'craggy, rugged' as well as 'tusked' and is
best known as the epithet of the legendary Brochwel Ysgithrog
– 'one of the grandsons of Brychan' - according to one source.

The present Scethrog House is not on the site of the older
residence of this n. which is what is now known as The Tower,
a 13th/14thC tower house.

**Slwch**                                               SO 0628
*Sloghe* 1488, *Slough or Slozthe* 1551,*The Slough* 1698, *Slwch* 1698,
*Slwch tump* 1813

ME *slo(u)gh* (from OE *slōh*), 'slough, quagmire'; the W form
preserves the 'fricative' E -*gh*-. Identical to Slough RAD in *A
Study of Radnorshire Place-Names*. The 1813 *tump* may refer to the
small hill-fort above Slwch (see Twmpa below).

**Storey Arms**                                         SN 9820
*Storey Arms* 1840

The n. of an outdoor education centre owing its n. to a Mr.
Storey who owned Forest Lodge (SN 9524), itself named
because it was a part of the Great Forest (see Fforest Fawr
above), in the first half of the 19thC. The present structure was
built c. 1930 as a youth hostel and replaced a small inn at SN
988199. The inn does not appear on the 1 in. OS map 1832 and
probably dates from about the time of the construction of the
Merthyr to Brecon turnpike road.

**Swydd Ddinan** cmt. Buellt, see **Llysdinam**

**Swydd Dreflys** see **Treflys**

**Swydd Irfon** (lost)
cmt. Buellt
*Soithervan, Soithirvon* 1424-5, *Southirven* 1550, *Southyrnon* 1360,
*South Irvon* 1553-8

W *swydd*, 'subdivision (or commote) of a cantref', and the rn.
*Irfon*; see Irfon above. A *swydd* in the cantref of Buellt, probably
identical to the commote of Is Irfon, 'below Irfon': *is Rivon* 1543,
*is irvon* c.1566, *Isyrwon* 1584. The other commotes were Swydd
Ddinan, Penbuellt and Treflys.

**Llyn Syfaddan** (Llan-gors Lake)                    SO 1326
*Brecenan Mere* 916 (=919), *Lake of Brekeniauc* c.1200, *Brechenauc mere . . . in Walche Llin Seuathan* 1536-9, *ynlinn Syuadon* c.1150, *llŷn syuadon* late 15thC, *Llynsavaddon* 1798, (lake) *Mara* late 12thC, *la Mare* 1327

The second largest natural lake in Wales, so well known that to some E writers it was simply *Brecknock Mere* (see the sps. above for 916 and 1536-9). To others it was simply 'the Mere' which is the meaning of *Mara*, a latinized form of ME *mere*. This is also found in *Mara langors* 1689, from its proximity to Llan-gors (above). William de *Mara*, who occurs 1127, may have taken his n. from the lake. The modern OS map form *Llangorse* (or rather *Llan-gors*) *Lake* seems to be a late n. The W n. has *llyn*, 'lake, pool', and *Syfaddan*, which has not been satisfactorily explained. The Celtic scholar John Rhŷs thought it might be a pers.n. related to Ir *Samthan*, the n. of a wicked princess, while Charles Thomas preferred to derive it from British *\*Samo-ton(a)*, a divine personification of the summer months (*\*samo-*), appropriately the best fishing period; *\*samo-*, however, produced ModW *haf*, 'summer', not *syf-*, *saf-*..

Gerald of Wales c.1191 calls it 'the great and famous lake of *Brecheniauc*, which some describe as *Clamosus*'. Latin *clamosus* means 'full of clamour or noise' and presumably refers to the 'horrible groaning noise' emitted by the ice when the lake was frozen in winter. but this explanation is likely to have arisen, according to Thomas Jones, through confusing *clamosus* with *calamosus*, 'reedy'; it cannot be coincidental that 'reeds' also occur in the pn. Llan-gors (above). The lake was said by Gerald to possess many remarkable characteristics including changing its colour from bright green to scarlet and the poet Higden has 'There is a pole at Breigheynok, There ynne of fische is many a flok; Ofte he chaunge his hewe on cop, And bere aboue a gardyn crop'. Camden c.1580 says that it had a drowning legend.

**Taf, Taf Fawr, Taf Fechan** rns.

*Tam, Taf maur, taf bechan* 12thC, *Taam, Taaph* c.1200, *Tamii fluminis* c.1140, *Tauus* 12thC, *Taue uaure,* ~ *uachan flu:* 1578, *TAF* 1102, *Greate Taf* 1583-4, *Taffe vawr* 1461, (places) *Tavehan* 12thC

Derived by Richards from *\*Tamios* or *Tabios*, though the first is likeliest in view of the sps. with *-m*. The n. is fairly common – we have *Taf* PEM – and similar rns. are found in other parts of Britain, such as *Team, Teme, Thame*, and the European continent. They were once thought by many authorities, to contain an el. *teme-*, 'dark', as in OIr *temen*, 'dark grey', but Jackson noted that darkness is 'not a very marked characteristic'. A better suggestion, made by Nicolaisen, is that they have Indo-European *\*tā̆* meaning 'to flow'.

**Talachddu**                                                    SO 0833
*Talachtu* 1263, *TALAUGH'DUY* 1400, *talachǒy* c.1566, *Talachdu* 1798, *Loughty* 1373

This may be *Tuchlarduveleys, Tuchlar Duueleys* 1241 but they would have to be very corrupt sps., perhaps for *\*Talachddu(f)lais*, where *Du(f)lais* is the nearby r. *Dulais*, 'black, dark stream', with *glais*, 'brook, stream'. If we accept this, then *Talachddu* might be a short form. *Talach-* remains difficult to explain; it might have W *tâl*, 'front, end', and *ach*, 'scar, line', in some topographical sense but there is nothing obvious here. The village lies on the line of the old road running from Bronllys through Felin-fach towards Llanddew.The sp. *Loughty* is a product of 'wrong division': initial *Ta-* or *Da-* has been confused with AF *de*, 'of', and dropped in copying.

**Talgarth**                                                    SO 1533
*Talgar* c.1163-74, *Talgard* c.1100, 1204-14, *Talgarth* c.1100, *kwmwd talgarth* c.1566, *Talgarth Ughporthe* 1569, *Talgarth Hewchporth* 1541-3 *English Tallgarthe* 1575, *Englysshe Talgarth* 1331, *INGLISSHE TALGARTH* 1520

Identical to *Talgarth* MTG, both meaning 'end of a ridge', with W *tâl*, 'forehead, front' and 'end, brow of a hill', and *garth*, 'mountain-ridge, promontory'; the ridge must be either the low promontory which extends north from Penywyrlodd (SO 153318) or that extending west from Rhos-fach (SO 1833) towards Talgarth.

*Talgarth* was the n. of a commote (*cwmwd*), covering the ps. of Cathedin, Llanelyw, Llan-gors and Talgarth. The lp. was divided into several manors: English Talgarth around Talgarth and Welsh Talgarth around Blaenllynfi castle (but excluding the castle itself). Some authorities add Tal-y-llyn. Talgarth Uwch Porth, 'Talgarth above the gate', included Llan-gors in 1569.

The church of Talgarth is now dedicated to Gwendoline but in 1488 it is *Sce Wenne Virginis*, explained as Gwen, 'granddaughter' of Brychan, and said to have been murdered by Saxons.

**Tal-y-bont (-on-Usk): Tal-y-bont (-ar-Wysg)** SO 1122
*Talpont* 14thC, *Talybont* 1560, 1754, *Tal y Bont* 1748, *Tal-y-bont* 1832

'End of the bridge', with *tal* as in Talgarth, def.art. *y* and *pont*, mutated after the def.art., describing a village at the west end of the bridge across the r. Caerfanell (*crafnell* 12thC, c.1400, *Carvanell* 1788, *Pont Krevannell* 1670-85). The modern forms with *on Usk* and *ar Wysg* use the r. Usk, about half-a-mile from the village, as a well-known landmark to distinguish it from other like pns. Tal-y-bont has given its n. to the reservoir about two miles above the village in Glyn Collwng.

**Tal y Fan** (lost: in lp. of Builth) forest
*Talvan* 1424-5, (forest, place) *Tallawyn* 1550

W *tal*, def.art. *y* and *ban*, mutated as *fan* after the def.art., meaning 'end of the peak'. Compare *Tal-y-fan* GLA which is *Thalevon, -van* 1248, *Talvan, Talevan* 1281.

**Tal-y-llyn**                                                    SO 1027
(manor) *Tale llyn* 1586-7, *Tallyn* 1372, 1600-7, (lp.) *Talyllyn*
17thC, (lp.) *TAL Y LLYNN* c.1600

The n. also survives in Llanfihangel Tal-y-llyn and Llangasty
Tal-y-llyn above. 'End of the lake', referring to Llyn Syfaddan
(Llan-gors Lake), though the hamlet is a very recent
development near the old tunnel on the Hay-Brecon tramroad.

**Tawe** rn.
*Tauuy* c.1150, *Tauy flu:* 1578, *Tavue* 12thC, *Loogh (Poole) Tawe,* (r.)
*Tawe* 1536-9

Richards explained it as derived from Brit *\*Tamouiā,* possibly
meaning 'water' (are not all rs. 'watery') or 'dark river' (but see
r. Taf above) while Ifor Williams favoured W *taw,* as in *tawel,*
'quiet, calm', with *gwy* (as in the rn. *Gwy/Wye*) which he
explains as 'bend, turn' and 'twisting'; *Tawy* might be 'quiet,
twisting (r.)'. *Tawe* is probably a late dialectical form; cf. *Olwy,
Olway* MON.

**Three Cocks** see Aberllynfi

**Tirabad**                                                       SN 8741
*Mickeland or tir yr Rubat, Nuckeland, otherwise Tir y rabat* 1623,
*Tyr yr abate* 1619, *Newchurch Tyr Abbott* 1821, *Newchurch or Tir
Abbott* 1828

'Abbot's land', with W *tir,* def.art. *yr* (now lost) and *abad,*
'abbot', referring to its former possession by the abbey of Strata
Florida CRD. *Nuckeland, Mickeland* must be copyist's errors for
*Munckeland,* 'Monkland'. *Newchurch* refers to the new church
built on a new site in 1716. Otherwise called *Llanddulas,* with
*glan* (not *llan*) and the rn. here *Dulas,* 'black stream' (*du* and
*glais,* 'brook, stream'), though Theophilus Jones says it was also
called *Aberdulas.* This is a farm at SN 916466 near the mouth of
the r. (with *aber,* 'confluence of two rivers, mouth of a river').

**Tir Ralff** (lost)

(commote) *Tyrrauf* 1294, (park) *Tyrrauf* 1301, *Comm. Tireraulf* 1536-9, *Tir Rrawlff* 1543, *Tir Raulff* 1584, (house at) *Tyraph'* 1292, *k. tir yr halff* c.1566

'Ralff's ~, Raff's land', with W *tir*, 'land, territory', and the AF pers.n. *Raulf*, probably Ralph Mortimer (died 1246) who married a daughter of Llywelyn the Great and widow of Reginald de Breos (died 1227-8) from whom he is said to have inherited the castle and lp. of Pencelli. Tir Ralff was the east division of Cantref Mawr, described as a commote in many sources.

**Torpantau** hill                    SO 0417

*Tor-pantau* 1832, *Tor-pantu* 1814

W *tor*, 'belly', related to Co *tor*, or *twr*, 'heap', and perhaps *pant(i)au*, pl. of *pant*, 'hollow, depression'.

**Traean-glas**

*Trayanglas* early 18thC, (hamlet) *TRAYAN-GLASE* 1804, *Trayan Glaes* 1743, *Traianglas* 1740

W *traean*, 'third', a division of a p. – in this case a chapel-of-ease to Llywel-like Traean-mawr below – and *glas*, 'green' (and 'blue').

**Traean-mawr**

*Trayan-mawr* early 18thC, *Traenmawr* 1753-4, *Trayan Mawr* 1743-80, (hamlet) *TRAYAN-MAWR* 1804

As Traean-glas, with *mawr*, 'big, greater'. The other 'third' of Llywel was Ysclydach below.

**Trallwng, Trallong**　　　　　　　　　　　　　SN 9629

*Tratlan* 1290, *Trallan* 1281, 1326 (1516), (manor) *Tralan* 1210-12, *Trathelan* 1361, *a thrallóng kynuyn* c.1180 (c.1300), *Trallionge* 1578, *Trallwng* 1283, *Trallonge* 1513, *TRATHLLONG* 1502

The dictionary of Thomas Richards of Coety explains *trallwng* as 'a soft place on the road (or elsewhere) as travellers may be apt to sink into, a dirty pool', ie. the intensive prefix *tra-* and *llwng*, 'wet'. It is fairly common, best known as the W n. of Welshpool MTG. In BRE, for example, we have the farm n. *Trallwm* (SN 877542) recorded as *i'r Trallwm* 1778, *Trallwng* 1833; in RAD there is *Cwm-trallwm* near Pen-y-bont and *Draenllwynbyr* (*y Tralhwghbyrr* late 16thC); in GLA there is *Trallwn*, a part of Pontypridd, near the r. Taf, and *Trallwn* at Swansea. Many sps. of these places have sps. with *-wm*, a feature of other words such as *carlwng*, *carlwm*, 'stoat'. OS maps spell this pn. *Trallong*, probably representing the 'wider' sound of *w*, rather like E *o* in 'bole', in some parts of south Wales. The pn. once had the addition of *Cynfyn*, perhaps the n. of a saint, though the church is now dedicated to Dewi/David.

**Trawsgoed**　　　　　　　　　　　　　　SN 9109, 9209

*y Troescoed* 1578, *Troscoed* 1795, *Troscoit, -coyt, -cote* 1372, *Pentre-tryscoed, Cefn-drys-coed* 1832

The sps. are similar to Trawsgoed (SO 084345), Llandyfalle, which is *Trosgoed* 1613, *Troescoed* 1801, *y Trosgoed* 1778, (hamlet) *TROESGOED* 1804; this may also be *Troscoit* 13thC where Dore abbey HER had a grange. Both have W *traws*, 'over, across', and *coed*, 'trees, wood', loosely 'wooded area'. The pn. is very common; there are examples near Llan-ŷr RAD, Guilsfield and Carno MTG, and CRD. The 1832 sps. above are corrupt but have unfortunately been transferred to modern maps.

**Trebarried** ho. SO 1135

*Trebaried* 1682-3, *Trebarried* 1767, *Tre-barried* 1832, *Trebarryed* 1657, *Trebaryed* 1600-1, (William Parry of) *Treberred* 1593

W *tref*, originally 'house, dwelling-place' as in this case, later 'hamlet, t., town', though the first meanings are implied by many other places in BRE and other W counties such as MTG. The second el. is uncertain. Attempts have been made to connect it with the n. of the reputed builder, William Parry or William ab Harry Vaughan, in the mid 17thC, with the implication that *-barried* is *Parriaid* or *Parried*, a pl. form of *Parry* found in pedigrees, but *-barried* is very reminiscent of the second el. in *Llwynbaried* (Llaneigon) which is *lloyne Berett* 1547-51 and *Llwyn-bered* 1832, and *Llwynbarried Hall*, Nantmel, RAD. If they contain the same el., it has yet to be convincingly explained. Melville Richards thought that *Trebarried, Trebared* (Cardigan) CRD and *Trebaried* (Llanfair-ar-y-bryn) CRM contained a pers.n. *Barret* and found the occurrence of Maurice and Walter *Bareth* at Cardigan in the 14thC significant. A pers.n. may well apply to one or both of these but can hardly explain them all. The sample is small but the occurrence of *-ba(r)ried* with *tref* and *llwyn* can hardly be fortuitous. Further research may solve the problem.

**Trebois (Boiston** (lost)) SO 1234

*Boyston, Boiston* 1380, *Treboys* 1684, 1698, *Trebois* 1843

W *tref* in its earlier sense of 'house, dwelling-place'. The earlier n. appears to have been *Boiston* with ME *-ton* matching W *tref*. The rest is said to have been the n. of a local family and Hugh Thomas, the historian, says that the lords of Trebois were descended from Sir Richard Bois, a follower of Bernard de Neufmarché, conqueror of Brycheiniog in the early 12thC, but there seems to be no reliable evidence to support this. It is likely to be a pers.n., possibly F *Bois* or *de Bois* as Thomas says, but it has also been explained as Old Germanic *Boio* or *Boia*. There are a number of similar pns. in this area having W *tref* combined with a pers.n., eg. Tregunter, Trehendre and Trephilip below.

**Trecastell, Trecastle**                                          SN 8829
*Trecastle* 1298, *Trecastel Toune* 1536-9, *Trecastell* 1778, *Trerecastell* 1569, *Trercastell* 1600-7

'Settlement by a castle', with W *tref* (as above) and *castell*, 'castle', referring to the motte-and-bailey, thought to be Norman, at its eastern end. The 1569 sp. suggests that the W def.art. *y*, affixed as *'r*, has been lost: that might explain the absence of any mutation (*c* to *g*) in *castell*. From 1276 to 1884 Trecastell was a detached ward of the Borough of Brecknock (Town) and, as such, some have speculated that the castle was that at Brecon.

**Tredomen**                                          SO 1231
*Tredomen* 1595, 1698, *Tre-domen* 1832

'Settlement by a mound', with *tref* as above and *tomen* (*tref* is fem. so *tomen* mutates to *domen*) 'mound', often 'castle mound'; there is a 'moat' at SN 119326. Tredomen Court is *Cwrt Tredomen* 1832, with W *cwrt* matching E *court*. See also Trephilip.

**Tredurn**                                          SO 1134
*Duynourton, Dynourton* 1380, *Tredyrne, al's Dynaston, al's Pont y Batte* 17thC, *Tredurn* c.1817

W *tref* as above and a pers.n. We know that Walter de *Duynr'* held half-a-fee in Brecknock and that Maurice de *Dynnor* was a tenant at Bronllys 1299 and it is very likely that they took their n. from *Dinedor* HER which occurs as *Durra* 1107-71, *Dunre* 1086, 1176 (and frequently) to the 15thC

*Pont-y-bat* is a distinct place: *Pont-y-bat* 1778, 1832, meaning 'bridge at the boat', perhaps referring to a 'boat' or ferry across the r. Dulas; there is now no bridge here nearer than that at SO

119339 but this was *Pont-gibal-fach* 1832, 'bridge at the little ferry', with *ceubal*, 'ferry', and *bach*, 'little'.

### Tredwstan SO 1432
*Turstenston* 14thC, *Dorstonstone* 1303, *Trefdurston otherwise Durstans Town* 1595, *Tredustin, -ton* 1574, *Tredwstan* 1778

B.G. Charles explained it as an OScand pers.n. *Thorsteinn* and OE *tūn*, meaning 'Thorsteinn's settlement'. The pers.n. is likely to be that of Turstan Bret who occurs in Brycheiniog late 12thC, Turstan *Seiher* 12thC and Walter Threstan c.1206-28. *Thorsteinn* was borrowed as OE *Thurstan* (*þurstān*) and was common in Normandy as *Troustin, Toustain*. The W form has replaced the older E one, translating *-ton* as *Tre(f)*, mutating *T-* to *-d-* (because *tref* is fem.) and reversing the consonant and vowel in the pers.n. *-urs-* to produce *-rws-* (nearly rhyming with E *goose*); the *-r-* was later lost.

Tredwstan was the site of an Independent chp. from 1668. See also Trephilip.

### Trefeca, Trefecca SO 1432
*Tre Vecca* c.1590-1610, *Trevecka* 1595, (ht.) *TREVECKA* 1804, *Tre-fecca-isaf, ~ -fawr* 1832, *Trevecta* 1574

This may also be *Trevek* 1398, known to have lain in Ystrad Yw lp. and *Traneck* (for *Traveck?*) 1309. W *tref* as above under Trebois and a ?pers.n., perhaps OE *Becca* as in *Beckley* SSX and *Beckbury* SHR but the sps. are very late. Tradition says it is named after *Rebecca* Prosser, presumably abbreviated as *Beca*. *Trefeca* PEM has similar past sps., although B.G. Charles, who has produced a lengthy examination of PEM pns., thought there was no connection in meaning.

Trefeca Fach, the site of today's Coleg Trefeca, is best known as the birthplace of Howel Harris (1714-73). Trefeca Isaf, now called College Farm, was where the Countess of Huntingdon built a college for the training of ministers of her 'Connexion' in 1768, but in 1792 it was moved to Cheshunt.

**Trefeinon**                                    SO 1330
*Trevinon* 1680, (manor) *Trevynon* 1781, *Trevythy al's Trevynon* 17thC, (farm) *Tref-einon* 1832

W *tref* as above and the pers.n. *Ein(i)on*

**Trefil**                                      SO 1212
*Tirfoel Lime Works*, ~ *Machine*, (hills) *Tirfoeldu*, ~ *Tir Foel Glas* 1814, (lands near) *y Truvill* 1704-7, (hills) *Trevill* 1766-69; *Trefil* 1832, (hills) *Trevil Du*, ~ *Glas* 1828; (hill) *Trevil Glas, or Tir voel glas* 1815

The stream here is *Nant Trefil* 1832 and the hills above have been feminized to *Trefil Ddu* and *Trefil Las*, with *du*, 'black, dark', and *glas*, 'green, blue'. Sps. are late and erratic and there are several possible meanings. If the original form is *Tir-foel*, 'bare, exposed land', this may have developed into *Tirfil* and *Trifil*, *Trefil*. Alternatively, we may have W *trafal*, *tryfal*, translated by Charles as 'triangle, land in a fork'. W *tryfal* is thought to occur in *Mathrafal*, *Trafel-gwyn* (SN 8975 at Llangurig) which lies in the fork of two streams, *Tryfel* (SN 9716 at Llangadfan) between Nant y Waun Fraith and Nant y Dwyslyn (*Nant Trafel* 1836), all in MTG, and *Travle* (SO 1742 at Llowes) BRE which is *Travelley* 1639. *Trefil Ddu* (Cwmcarfan) MON was *Trevellddey* 1600-7 and there is also a reference to a *Treveldee* near Monmouth in deeds 1646-1756.

**Trefithel**                                   SO 1536
*Ytheleston* 1380, *Ithelston* 14thC, *Trevethell* 1521, *Terwythell* 1533-8, *Trevithel* 1608, 1832, *Trevithell* 1624

'Ithel's settlement'; despite the 1380 sp., W *tref* may be the original generic in this pn., because the pers.n. W. *Ithel* occurs in *Pontithel* (SO 165369), ½ mile east of Trefithel; Edward Lhuyd, scientist and scholar, c.1700 calls it *Pont Ithel*.

147

**Treflys**                                                              SN 9349

(reeve of) *Treslees* (= *Treflees*) 1424-5, *Trefles* 1360, *Treflays* 1547, *Trevlys* 1553-8, *Trefflys* 1360-7, (commote) *Dreulys* 1584, *Keven Treflys* 1533-8, *s. drevlys* 1543, *swydd dreflys* c.1560-66

W *tref* as above and *llys* (as in Llys-wen above), meaning 'settlement with a court'. The 'court' may well be the administrative centre of *Swydd Dreflys*, 'court of Treflys', with *swydd*, 'sitting, court', alias the commote of Treflys. Both commote and *swydd* were applied to subdivisions of a cantref, in this case Buellt (see Builth).

**Tre-goed, Tregoyd**                                                    SO 1937

*Trefgoit, -goyt* 1380, *Tregoed* 1600-7, 1640, 1832, *Tregoide* 1522, *Tregoyd* 1828

'Settlement with a wood', with W *tref* and *coed*, trees, wood'. Edward Lhuyd c.1700 gives the sp. *Tre Gôd* (with a long *o* sound like E *o* in 'code'); W *-oe-* is often pronounced this way in south Wales. There is an identical pn. in RAD; see *A Study of Radnorshire Place-Names*, p.92.

**Tregunter**                                                            SO 1333

*Gunterston* 1403, *Tregunter* 1595, 1782, 1798, *Tref Gwnter late* 15thC, *Tre Gunter* 1832

'Gunter's settlement', with W *tref*, probably replacing ME *-ton* which had an identical meaning, and a pers.n. of continental Germanic origin, borrowed in F as *Gontier*. According to Hugh Thomas and Theophilus Jones the manor of Gunterston was granted to Sir Peter Gunter by Bernard de Neufmarché, conquereror of Brycheiniog. That remains unproven but the n. certainly occurs in early charters relating to Brecon priory, eg. Robert son of Gunter late 12thC. For other examples of W *tref* replacing ME *-ton*, see Tredurn, Tredwstan and Trehendre.

**Trehendre** SO 0934

*Henryston* 14thC, *Hareston* 1566, 1567, *Hieston* [=*Harieston?*]
*vocat' Lake* 1380, *Trehenre* 1522, *Trehenry-fawr,* ~ *-fach* c.1817, *Tre
Henry-fawr,* ~ *-fach* 1832

W *tref,* replacing ME *-ton* (see Tregunter above), and OF *Henri,*
borrowed from OG *Haimric, Henric,* meaning 'home rule'. In E it
became *Henry, Hendry* and *Harry* (as in the 1566 sp.); sps. such
as *Hendry* may have encouraged the late confusion with W
*hendre(f),* literally 'old settlement', with the particular meaning
of 'winter dwelling' (testimony of transhumance – as opposed
to the *hafod* or 'summer dwelling', usually in the hills). For *Lake,*
see Cwrtllaca which is about half-a-mile away.

**Trephilip** SO 1234

*Phelippes-, Philippeston* 1380, *Trephilip* 1513, *Tre Philip* 1832, *Tref
ph'* late 15thC, *Trefullit* 1760

This may be *Tref ph'* referred to by the poet Lewys Glyn Cothi
1447-89 in his 'Moliant ['Praise of'] Ieuan ap Gwilym Fychan'.
W *tref,* replacing ME *-ton* (see Trehendre, etc. above), and the
pers.n., reputedly that of a Philip ap John Lawrence Bullen. The
pns. Tredomen, Tredwstan and Trephilip in this locality are all
within a mile radius of each other and all are duplicated near
Defynnog (at SN 9227). This cannot be coincidental and it is
generally agreed that they recall the practice of farmers moving
their stock up into the hills in summer time.

**Tre'resgob: Bishop's Town** SN 8729

*Bisshops Toun* 1536-9, *Tref Esgob* 1706-35, *Tre'r Esgob or
Bishopstone* 1809

The W n. is a literal translation of the E. This settlement now
forms part of the modern village of Trecastell (see above) but in
medieval times it had a separate status under the Bishop of St.
David's under whom it remained until the Reformation.

**Tre-twˆr, Tretower**                                      SO 1821

*Trevetour 1463, Treretower 1557, Trertowre 1600-7, Tretour 1520,*
*Tretowre 1578, 1600-7, Tref y Twr 1534-80, tre r t6r late 15thC*

'The tower settlement', with W *tref, tre,* as above and *tˆwr,* a
borrowing from ME *tour,* ModE *tower.* Some W sps. suggest
that a def.art. *y,* '*r* has been lost, ie. *Tre'r-tˆwr.* No doubt
familiarity with *tower* helped to preserve the rather odd sp. still
found on maps as *Tretower.* The 'tower' was the castle, probably
established by a certain Picard in the late 11thC, since it is later
found in the custody of his descendants. It is best known for
Tretower Court, the medieval mansion, built in the 14thC.

**Trewalkin**                                               SO 1531

*villam Walkelini 1206-28, Walkyngeston 1535, Trewalkyn 1574, Tre*
*Walkin 1532, Tir Peter Gunter alias Trewalkin 1769*

W *tref* replacing ME *-ton* as in Tredurn, Tredwstan, Tregunter,
Trehendre and Trephilip above and Troed-yr-harn below, with
AF *Walchelin,* a diminutive of OG *Walho* or *Walico* according to
DES (under *Wakelin*). There are refs. in local charters to land
formerly held by Walkelin Vis de Lu of Penllanafel (SO 156296)
c.1143-54 and his land 'between the lake [probably Llyn
Syfaddan] and the earthwork of Walkelin' late 12thC.
Trewalkin is about 3 miles from Llyn Syfaddan (Llan-gors
Lake).

**Trewalter**                                               SO 1229

*Trewalter apud Durstanton 1503, Walterstone Goch c.1322-3, Tre-*
*walter 1832,* (forest) *Watersland* (in Cantref Selyf) 1566, *Trewalter*
*Gough otherwise ~ Goch, Trewalter farm 1805*

W *tref* replacing ME *-ton* (see Trewalkin), and pers.n. *Walter,* OG
meaning 'mighty army', borrowed as F *Gautier,* E *Walter. Goch*
c.1322-3 has W *coch* mutated as *goch,* 'red, crimson', perhaps
referring to the colour of the soil or even the buildings. There is
a *Trewalter Wen,* 'white, fair Trewalter', in PEM which occurs as

*Walteryston* 1406, *Trewallter* 1573 and a *Walterston* HER. For *Durstanton*, see Tredwstan.

**Troed-yr-harn: Tredrahaearn**                    SO 0630
*Traharneston* 1372, *Troed-yr-harn* 1832, *Trauston'* 1453, *llys Trahaern llwyd* c.1500

At Llan-ddew. There is an identical pn. at Talgarth (SO 1632) which is *Traharneston* 1331, *Tredyrhoyrne* 1574, *Troed r harn* 1832, *Troed-yr-harn* 1828. In both cases W *tref* and ME *-ton* as in Trewalkin, Trewalter etc., and a W pers.n. *Trahaearn*, mutated as *-drahaearn*. Alice *Traharn* occurs at Llan-gors 1331; *Trahaearn* ap Madog held part of Brycheiniog between 1262 and 1276; a *Traar* ap Eynon was a tenant in the lp. of Brecknock 1299; and a Thomas ap *Traharn* occurs here in 1372. The pers.n. may contain W *tra*, 'over, excessive', and *haearn*, 'iron', perhaps in the sense of 'powerful'. In both cases *Tredrahaearn* has become confused with W *troed*, 'foot', def.art. *yr* and *haearn*, 'iron'; *troed* is a common pn. el. used to mean a place 'at the foot' of something, eg. *Troed-y-rhiw* GLA, 'at the foot of the slope'.

**Twmpa** hill                                     SO 2235

No sps. seen; on the OS 2 in. map drawings 1816-17 it is shown with Darren Lwyd bearing the n. *Mynydd Trwyntal*. Probably W *twmpa(th)* or *twmpau* as pl. of *twmp*, a W borrowing from late ME *tump, tompe*, 'small hillock, mound', applying to the summit of Darren Lwyd overlooking the Wye valley. *Darren Lwyd* itself has W *tarren*, mutated after a lost def.art. *y*, 'knoll, rock, tump, prominent rock', and *llwyd*, 'grey, brown' etc.

**Twyn Du** hill                                   SO 0820
*Twyn-du* 1832

'Black hill', with W *twyn*, 'hill, hillock, tump, knoll', and *du*, 'black, dark'. The n. is now applied to a hill slope but on the OS

1 in. map 1832 it describes more appropriately the hill on the north side of Nant Tarthwyni. The last has W *nant*, 'stream' (earlier 'valley'), *tarth*, 'mist', *gwyn*, 'white, fair', with a suffix –*i*, 'stream like white mist'?

### Twyn Rhyd-car hill           SN 9642
*Twyn-rhyd-caer* 1832, *Twyn rhyd Cier* c.1817

W *twyn* as in Twyn Du above, *rhyd*, 'ford', and *car* probably meaning and referring to the 'stream' Ysgir Fechan which had the settlements Blaen-car (lost), Car, Cwm-car alongside and Rhyd-car (lost) close by. Compare Maes-car above. The change of *car* to *caer*, 'fort', occurs in other pns. but in this case there is no evidence of any such antiquity.

### Tyn-y-graig           SO 0149
*Ty'n-y-graig* 1817, 1833

'Small farm at the rock', with W *tyddyn*, *tyn*, def.art. *y* and *craig*, mutated as *graig*, 'rock, cliff'. Tyn-y-graig stands at the east end of a steep slope and close to the deeply-incised course of the r. Cneiddon.

### Upper Chapel see Capel Dyffryn Honddu

### Usk: Wysg rn.
*Osce* c.1100, *in aquam Oschæ flumine* c.1191, *Vsc* 1204-14, *uysc* c.1150, *Uscha* c.1100, *Husca* 1143-54, (water of) *Husk'* 1326 (1516), *Wisch, Uske* 1536-9

Probably 'r. abounding in fish'. ModW *Wysg* derives from OW *Uisc* and ultimately from Brit *\*Ēscā̆, Ēiscā̆*; a related word has produced OIr *iasc*, 'fish'. The Roman fort of Caerleon near the mouth of the r. Usk occurs as *ISCA* in the Ravenna Cosmography c.700 but the sp. is likely to have been influenced by spoken Latin.

**Uwchdyfnant** (lost)                                                SN ?8312, 8415, etc.
*Eughedeuenant in Glyntawy* 1372, *Ughdeuenant* 1454, (village called) *Dynfant* 1801, *Dunfant* 1829

W *uwch*, 'above, higher', and *Dyfnant* (SN 8212), a former village now part of modern Aber-craf (SN 8112-8212). *Dyfnant* has *dwfn* and *nant* meaning 'deep stream or ravine' and refers to Nant Craf. The two early refs. seem to apply to part of Ystradgynlais Higher above Aber-craf. Later sps. show the change ('metathesis') of *Dyfnant* to *Dynfant* as in the case of *Dunvant*, properly *Dynfant* GLA (near Swansea), which occurs as *Dyffnant* 1652, *Dyvnant* 1736-65 and *Dunvant* 1833.


**Vaynor** see **Faenor**


**Velindre** see **Felindre**


**Waun Fach** hill                                                          SO 2129
*Waun-fach* 1832

W *gwaun*, 'high and west level ground, moorland, heath', and *bach*, mutated as *fach* because *gwaun* is fem. The n. must indicate 'small moor' in comparison with some other local moor rather than the hill because it is the highest (2660 ft.) in the Black Mountain. The 'other moor' may be on Mynydd Llysiau (SO 2027); the OS 2in. scale map drawings 1816-17 misapply *Waun Mynyddllysiau* to Waun-fach (see Mynydd Llysiau above).


**Waun Lysiog** hill                                                        SN 0116
*Gwaun-llyseuog* 1832, *Waun llysieuog* 1814

A mountain slope; on the south side are the valley Cwm Llysiog (*Cwm-llyseuog* 1832) with its stream Afon Llysiog (*Afon Llyseuog* 1814) and an area at its head Ffynnon Llysiog. The common el. may be *llyseuog*, 'herbaceous', and *gwaun* (as in Waun-fach above); *cwm* is 'deep, narrow valley, coomb'; *ffynnon* in this context means 'r. source'. The modern sp. *Llysiog* appears to show the influence of *llus*, 'whinberries, bilberries'.

**Weynard's Castle** (lost) antiquity                    SO ?1529
*castellum Weynardi* c.1143-54, ~ *Weinardi* late 12thC

Carn y Castell, 'the castle cairn', because the first ref. above says that land late of Walkelin Vis de Lu (see Trewalkin above) of Penllanafel (*Pentenauel*) extended to *castellum Weynardi*. Penllanafel is about a mile from Carn y Castell. Coplestone-Crow (*Brycheiniog 26*) identified the castle with Cefn Barn motte (SO 145314).

**River Wye: Afon Gwy** see *A Study of Radnorshire Place-Names*, p.95.

**Ynysgedwyn**                                      SN 7709
*Enys Kedwyn* 1510, *Tyr Enys Gedwyn* 1558, *Yniskedwin* 1648, 1754, *Ynyscedwyn* c.1814-20, *Ynys-cedwyn Sta.* 1886

'Cedwyn's water-meadow', with *ynys*, which also means 'island', and a pers.n., properly mutated as *Gedwyn* because *ynys* is a fem. n. There is no substance to the suggestion of Poole 1886 that it contains the n. of Edwain son of Einion son of Owain. The pers.n. is found in early W genealogies as *Kedwyn*, *Ketwyn*, though they are unconnected with this place. The large house and farm of this n. was occupied by the Awbrey and Gough families from the 17thC to 1933 when it became a Council depot; it was demolished in 1998. It gave its n. to the nearby ironworks (17thC to 1942) and later a collliery, both giving rise to settlements.

**Ysclydach, Sclydach** (lost)                        SN 9030
*Ysclidach* 1754, (hamlet) *YSGLYDACK* 1804, *Sclydach or Is-clydach* 1809

Probably *ys* from *is*, 'under, below, lower (down) than', and the rn. *Clydach* (see above), aptly describing its location, but the sps. are late and it is just possible that it might also mean 'river-meadow by r. Clydach' containing W *ynys*, 'river-meadow' (as well as 'island'). The pn. may have been 'wrongly-divided', ie. an original *Ynysclydach* might have been understood as *yn Ysclydach* ('in Ysclydach') and *Y-* would be lost in the same manner as in *ysgubor*, *'sgubor* and *ystafell*, *'stafell* in spoken W, to produce *Sclydach*. There are similar cases in other parts of Wales, eg. *Sketty* or rather *Sgeti* GLA from *Ynysgeti* and *Skenfrith* MON from *Ynysgynwraidd* (both containing pers.ns.).

**Ysgir** see **Aberysgir**

**Ystradcallwen** see **Callwen**

**Ystradfellte**                                     SN 9313
*Estradvelt, Istradvelt* 1559, *Istradwelthye* 1578, *Stradenetle* 1295, (constable of) *Stratmelthin* 1230, *ystrad felle de* c.1566, *Ystradfellte* early 16thC, *Ystrad-fellte* 1832, *Ystradvelltau* 1828, *Strathvelthly* 1316, *Ystrat Vellte* 1537

W *ystrad*, 'vale, valley-bottom', related to Breton *strad* and Ir *srath*, 'river valley', with the rn. *Mellte*. This is *melltou, Melldou* 12thC, *Mellte* 1578, 1832, containing W *mellt*, 'lightning' (probably alluding to the spectacular waterfalls on its course) and *tou, teu, te* seen also in its tributary *Hepste, Hebsteu*, thought to mean 'dark' (see Taf above) (alluding to the cavern Porth yr Ogof through which the r. flows for part of its course). There was also a pers.n. *Mellte* (possibly containing *mell*, 'mild, gentle, pleasant') thought to occur in *Bedwellty* MON. In a 13thC manuscript called 'De Situ Brecheniauc', there is a mention of the stone of Mellte (*Meltheu*) under which were said to lie the remains of Hunydd, daughter of Brychan. It would be very easy to connect this with the rn. Mellte in view of the ref. to Brychan but there are no clues to its location.

**Ystradgynlais**  SN 7810

(church) *Strangedeles* 1397, *Stradgenles* 1373, *ESTRATGYNLES* 1493, *Istradgynles* 1578, *ystrat gynleis* late 15thC, *Ystraedgynlais* 1798

W *ystrad* as in Ystradfellte above and the rn. *Cynlais* evidenced as *Cingleis, blayn cygleis* 1129, *Kyn-leic* 1510, *Genles, a little ryver* 1536-9, *Gurlais* 1833 and *Nant Gyrlais* on modern maps. The last sp. is probably based on the farm ns. which have this rn. although there is no uniformity in their sps. The second el. of the rn. might contain W *glais*, 'brook, stream', changing to *-lais* after the adj. *cynt, cyn*, 'faster, swifter'. Another possibility, common in rns., is a pers.n, in this case *Cynlas*, found as *Cinglas, Cuneglasus* in several medieval genealogical tracts. Theophilus Jones explained the pers.n. as that of *Gunleus* ap Glywysing (he spells this *Glewissig*), a fictitious prince of Gwent. Jones even gives the church dedication as *Gunleus* but it was *Cynog* in 1836.

**Ystrad Yw** cantref

*estrateu* 12thC, (church of) *Stratden'* c.1291, *Stradewi* 1140-50, (forest of) *Stradewi* 1121, *Straddewy* c.1234, 1331, (manor, castle of) *Straddeuwy alias Straddewy* 1306, *k. ystrad dyw ucha, ~ issa* c.1566, *Inistratyw* 12thC

This may also be *Ystradvi* c.1102-5 (c.1250). W *ystrad*, as in Ystradfellte and Ystradgynlais above, and a rn. *Yw* which rises at *Llygadwy* (SO 150213). This is *Llygad-yw* 1832, literally 'eye of Yw', meaning 'source of Yw'. Phillimore, the eminent philologist, thought that the rn. must be W *yw*, pl. of *ywen*, 'yew-tree', but it is called *Ewyn* 1832 and nearly all early sps. have *-ewi, -ewy, -wi* and *-dewi* and W sps. with *Yw* are generally late. Early sps. rule out W *ewyn*, 'foam', as the meaning of the rn. and it really deserves further investigation. It is unlikely to be W *dwy(w)*, 'God', as in *Dyfrdwy* (r. Dee) because the *-d* in *ystrad* and *d-* of *dwy(w)* would produce *-t-* when they meet.

The cantref of Ystrad Yw was divided into two commotes

Ystrad Yw Uchaf ('upper') and ~ Isaf ('lower'). The church in the c.1291 ref. above is Llanfihangel Cwm Du above.